new interchange

English for international communication

Jack C. Richards

with Jonathan Hull and Susan Proctor

student's book

1A

New Interchange Student's Book revision prepared by Jack C. Richards.

CAMBRIDGE
UNIVERSITY PRESS

PUBLISHED BY THE PRESS SYNDICATE OF THE UNIVERSITY OF CAMBRIDGE
The Pitt Building, Trumpington Street, Cambridge, United Kingdom

CAMBRIDGE UNIVERSITY PRESS
The Edinburgh Building, Cambridge CB2 2RU, UK
40 West 20th Street, New York, NY 10011–4211, USA
477 Williamstown Road, Port Melbourne, VIC 3207, Australia
Ruiz de Alarcón 13, 28014 Madrid, Spain
Dock House, The Waterfront, Cape Town 8001, South Africa

http://www.cambridge.org

First published 1997
12th printing 2002

New Interchange Student's Book 1 has been developed from *Interchange* Student's Book 1,
first published by Cambridge University Press in 1990.

Printed in Hong Kong, China

Typeface New Century Schoolbook   *System* QuarkXPress®   [AH]

A catalog record for this book is available from the British Library

Library of Congress Cataloging in Publication data
Richards, Jack C.
New interchange: English for international communication :
student's book 1 / Jack C. Richards with Jonathan Hull and Susan Proctor.
p.   cm.
Rev. ed. of: Interchange : English for international communication :
student's book 1. 1990.
ISBN 0-521-62881-4
1. English language – Textbooks for foreign speakers.
2. Communication, International – Problems, exercises, etc.
I. Hull, Jonathan. II. Proctor, Susan. III. Richards,
Jack C. Interchange. IV. Title.
PE1128.R459   1997
428.2'4 – dc21   97-17432
                                                                    CIP

ISBN 0 521 62881 4 Student's Book 1
ISBN 0 521 62880 6 Student's Book 1A
ISBN 0 521 62879 2 Student's Book 1B
ISBN 0 521 62878 4 Workbook 1
ISBN 0 521 62877 6 Workbook 1A
ISBN 0 521 62876 8 Workbook 1B
ISBN 0 521 62875 X Teacher's Edition 1
ISBN 0 521 62874 1 Teacher's Manual 1
ISBN 0 521 62873 3 Class Audio Cassettes 1
ISBN 0 521 62871 7 Student's Audio Cassette 1A
ISBN 0 521 62869 5 Student's Audio Cassette 1B
ISBN 0 521 62872 5 Class Audio CDs 1
ISBN 0 521 62870 9 Student's Audio CD 1A
ISBN 0 521 62868 7 Student's Audio CD 1B
ISBN 0 521 95019 8 Audio Sampler 1–3

Also available
ISBN 0 521 62867 9 Video 1 (NTSC)
ISBN 0 521 62866 0 Video 1 (PAL)
ISBN 0 521 62865 2 Video 1 (SECAM)
ISBN 0 521 62864 4 Video Activity Book 1
ISBN 0 521 62863 6 Video Teacher's Guide 1
ISBN 0 521 63887 9 Video Sampler 1–2
ISBN 0 521 62667 6 CD-ROM (PC format)
ISBN 0 521 62666 8 CD-ROM (Mac format)

Forthcoming
ISBN 0 521 62882 2 Placement Test (revised)
ISBN 0 521 77381 4 Lab Guide 1
ISBN 0 521 77380 6 Lab Cassettes 1

Available from the First Edition
ISBN 0 521 46759 4 Placement Test
ISBN 0 521 42218 3 Lab Guide 1
ISBN 0 521 42217 5 Lab Cassettes 1

Book design, art direction, and layout services: Adventure House, NYC
Illustrators: Adventure House, Barbara Griffel, Randy Jones, Mark Kaufman, Kevin Spaulding, Sam Viviano
Photo researcher: Sylvia P. Bloch

Introduction

THE NEW EDITION

New Interchange is a revision of *Interchange*, one of the world's most successful and popular English courses. *New Interchange* incorporates many improvements suggested by teachers and students from around the world. Some major changes include many new Conversations, Snapshots, and Readings; more extensive Grammar Focus models and activities; a greater variety and amount of listening materials; extensive changes to the **Teacher's Edition** and **Workbook**; and additions to the **Video**.

New Interchange is a multi-level course in English as a second or foreign language for young adults and adults. The course covers the four skills of listening, speaking, reading, and writing, as well as improving pronunciation and building vocabulary. Particular emphasis is placed on listening and speaking. The primary goal of the course is to teach communicative competence, that is, the ability to communicate in English according to the situation, purpose, and roles of the participants. The language used in *New Interchange* is American English; however, the course reflects the fact that English is the major language of international communication and is not limited to any one country, region, or culture. This level is for beginners and takes students from the beginning to low-intermediate level.

This level builds on the foundations for accurate and fluent communication already established in the prior level by extending grammatical, lexical, and functional skills. Because the syllabus covered in this Student's Book reviews language features taught at the prior level, students who have not previously used *New Interchange* can successfully study at this level.

COURSE LENGTH

Each full level of *New Interchange* contains between 70 and 120 hours of class instruction time. For classes where more time is available, the Teacher's Edition gives detailed suggestions for Optional Activities to extend each unit.

Where less time is available, the amount of time spent on Interchange Activities, Reading, Writing, Optional Activities, and the Workbook can be reduced.

Each split edition contains approximately 35 to 60 hours of classroom material. The Student's Book, Workbook, and Student's Audio Cassettes or CDs are available in split editions.

COURSE COMPONENTS

The **Student's Book** contains 16 six-page units, each divided into two topical/functional "cycles," as well as four review units. At the back of the book are 16 communication tasks, called "Interchange Activities," and summaries of grammar and vocabulary taught in each unit.

The full-color **Teacher's Edition** features detailed teaching instructions directly across from the Student's Book pages, along with audio scripts, cultural notes, answer keys, and optional activities. At the back of the Teacher's Edition are instructions for Interchange Activities, an Optional Activities Index, a Workbook Answer Key, and four photocopiable Achievement Tests with audio scripts and answer keys.

The **Workbook** provides a variety of reading, writing, and spelling exercises to reinforce the grammar and vocabulary taught in the Student's Book. Each six-page unit follows the same teaching sequence as the Student's Book; some exercises recycle teaching points from previous units in the context of the new topic. The Workbook can be used for classwork or homework.

The **Class Audio Program**, available on cassette or CD, is intended for classroom use. The Conversations, Grammar Focus models, Pronunciation exercises, and Listening activities in the Student's Book are all recorded naturally with a variety of native and some nonnative accents. Recorded exercises are indicated with the symbol ▭◉.

The **Student's Audio Program** provides opportunities for self-study. It contains recordings of all Student's Book exercises marked with the symbol ☁♪, except for the Listening tasks, which are intended only for classroom use. These tasks appear exclusively on the Class Audio Program and are indicated by the symbol ▶CLASS AUDIO ONLY.

The **Video** offers entertaining dramatic or documentary sequences that review and extend language learned in each unit of the Student's Book. The **Video Activity Book** contains comprehension, conversation, and language practice activities, and the **Video Teacher's Guide** provides instructional support, answer keys, and photocopiable transcripts of the video sequences.

The **CD-ROM**, appropriate for home or laboratory use, offers a wealth of additional practice. Each of the 16 units is based on a sequence from the Video. Four tests help students monitor their progress.

The **Placement Test** helps determine the most appropriate level of *New Interchange* for incoming students. A booklet contains the four-skills test on photocopiable pages, as well as instructions for test administration and scoring. A cassette accompanies the listening section of the test.

The **Lab Cassettes** provide self-study activities in the areas of grammar, vocabulary, pronunciation, listening, and functional use of English. The **Lab Guide** contains photocopiable pages that guide students through the activities.

The **Teacher-Training Video** offers clear guidance for teaching each section of the Student's Book and professional development activities appropriate for individual or group use.

■ APPROACH AND METHODOLOGY

New Interchange teaches students to use English for everyday situations and purposes related to school, social life, work, and leisure. The underlying philosophy is that learning a second or foreign language is more rewarding, meaningful, and effective when the language is used for authentic communication. Throughout *New Interchange,* students are presented with natural and useful language. In addition, students have the opportunity to personalize the language they learn, make use of their own knowledge and experiences, and express their ideas and opinions.

■ KEY FEATURES

Adult and International Content *New Interchange* deals with contemporary topics that are of high interest and relevant to both students and teachers. The topics have been selected for their interest to both homogeneous and heterogeneous classes.

Integrated Syllabus *New Interchange* has an integrated, multi-skills syllabus that links topics, communicative functions, and grammar. Grammar – seen as an essential component of second and foreign language proficiency and competence – is always presented communicatively, with controlled accuracy-based activities leading to fluency-based communicative practice. In this way, there is a link between grammatical form and communicative function. The syllabus is carefully graded, with a gradual progression of teaching items.

Enjoyable and Useful Learning Activities A variety of interesting and enjoyable activities provides thorough individual student practice and enables learners to apply the language they learn. The course also makes extensive use of information-gap tasks; role plays; and pair, group, and whole class activities. Task-based and information-sharing activities provide a maximum amount of student-generated communication.

■ WHAT EACH UNIT CONTAINS

Snapshot The Snapshots graphically present interesting real-world information that introduces the topic of a unit or cycle, and also develop vocabulary. Follow-up questions encourage discussion of the Snapshot material and personalize the topic.

Conversation The Conversations introduce the new grammar of each cycle in a communicative context and present functional and conversational expressions.

Grammar Focus The new grammar of each unit is presented in color boxes and is followed by controlled and freer communicative practice activities. These freer activities often have students use the grammar in a personal context.

Fluency Exercise These pair, group, whole class, or role-play activities provide more personal practice of the new teaching points and increase the opportunity for individual student practice.

Pronunciation These exercises focus on important features of spoken English, including stress, rhythm, intonation, reductions, and blending.

Listening The Listening activities develop a wide variety of listening skills, including listening for gist, listening for details, and inferring meaning from context. Charts or graphics often accompany these task-based exercises to lend support to students.

Word Power The Word Power activities develop students' vocabulary through a variety of interesting tasks, such as word maps and collocation exercises. Word Power activities are usually followed by oral or written practice that helps students understand how to use the vocabulary in context.

Writing The Writing exercises include practical writing tasks that extend and reinforce the teaching points in the unit and help develop student's compositional skills. The Teacher's Edition demonstrates how to use the models and exercises to focus on the process of writing.

Reading The reading passages use various types of texts adapted from authentic sources. The Readings develop a variety of reading skills, including reading for details, skimming, scanning, and making inferences. Also included are pre-reading and post-reading questions that use the topic of the reading as a springboard to discussion.

Interchange Activities The Interchange Activities are pair work, group work, or whole class activities involving information sharing and role playing to encourage real communication. These exercises are a central part of the course and allow students to extend and personalize what they have practiced and learned in each unit.

Unit Summaries Unit Summaries are located at the back of the Student's Book. They contain lists of the key vocabulary and functional expressions, as well as grammar extensions for each unit.

■ FROM THE AUTHORS

We hope that you will like using *New Interchange* and find it useful, interesting, and fun. Our goal has been to provide teachers and students with activities that make the English class a time to look forward to and, at the same time, provide students with the skills they need to use English outside the classroom. Please let us know how you enjoy it and good luck!

Jack C. Richards
Jonathan Hull
Susan Proctor

Authors' Acknowledgments

A great number of people contributed to the development of *New Interchange*. Particular thanks are owed to the following:

The **reviewers** using the first edition of *Interchange* in the following schools and institutes – the insights and suggestions of these teachers and their students have helped define the content and format of the new edition: Jorge Haber Resque, **Centro Cultural Brasil-Estados Unidos (CCBEU),** Belém, Brazil; Lynne Roecklein, **Gifu University,** Japan; Mary Oliveira and Montserrat M. Djmal, **Instituto Brasil-Esatdos Unidos (IBEU),** Rio de Janeiro, Brazil; Liliana Baltra, **Instituto Chileno Norte-Americano,** Santiago de Chile; Blanca Arazi and the teachers at **Instituto Cultural Argentino Norteamericano (ICANA),** Buenos Aires, Argentina; Mike Millin and Kelley Seymour, **James English School,** Japan; Matilde Legorreta, **Kratos, S.A. de C.V.,** Mexico D.F.; Peg Donner, Ricia Doren, and Andrew Sachar, **Rancho Santiago College Centennial Education Center,** Santa Ana, California, USA; James Hale, **Sundai ELS,** Japan; Christopher Lynch, **Sunshine College,** Tokyo,

Japan; Valerie Benson, **Suzugamine Women's College,** Hiroshima, Japan; Michael Barnes, **Tokyu Be Seminar,** Japan; Claude Arnaud and Paul Chris McVay, **Toyo Women's College,** Tokyo, Japan; Maria Emilia Rey Silva, **UCBEU,** São Paulo, Brazil; Lilia Ortega Sepulveda, **Unidad Lomoa Hermosa,** Mexico D.F.; Eric Bray, **Kyoto YMCA English School,** Kyoto, Japan; John Pak, **Yokohama YMCA English School,** Yokohama, Japan; and the many teachers around the world who responded to the *Interchange* questionnaire.

The **editorial** and **production** team: Suzette André, Sylvia P. Bloch, John Borrelli, Mary Carson, Natalie Nordby Chen, Karen Davy, Randee Falk, Andrew Gitzy, Pauline Ireland, Penny Laporte, Kathy Niemczyk, Kathleen Schultz, Rosie Stamp, and Mary Vaughn.

And Cambridge University Press **staff** and **advisors**: Carlos Barbisan, Kate Cory-Wright, Riitta da Costa, Peter Davison, Peter Donovan, Cecilia Gómez, Colin Hayes, Thares Keeree, Jinsook Kim, Koen Van Landeghem, Carine Mitchell, Sabina Sahni, Helen Sandiford, Dan Schulte, Ian Sutherland, Chris White, and Ellen Zlotnick.

Plan of Book 1A

Title/Topics	Functions	Grammar
UNIT 1 — PAGES 2–7		
Please call me Chuck. Introductions and greetings; names and titles; countries and nationalities	Introducing yourself; introducing someone; checking information; asking about someone; exchanging personal information	Wh-questions and statements with *be*; yes/no questions and short answers with *be*; contractions; subject pronouns; possessive adjectives
UNIT 2 — PAGES 8–13		
How do you spend your day? Occupations, workplaces, and school; daily schedules; clock time	Describing work and school; asking for and giving opinions; talking about daily schedules	Simple present Wh-questions and statements; time expressions: *at, in, on, around, until, before, after, early,* and *late*
UNIT 3 — PAGES 14–19		
How much is it? Spending habits, shopping, and prices; clothing and personal items; colors and materials	Talking about prices; giving opinions; talking about preferences; making comparisons; buying and selling things	Demonstratives: *this, that, these, those; one* and *ones*; questions: *how much* and *which*; comparisons with adjectives
UNIT 4 — PAGES 20–25		
Do you like jazz? Music, movies, TV programs; entertainers; invitations and excuses; dates and times	Talking about likes and dislikes; giving opinions; making invitations and excuses	Simple present yes/no and Wh-questions with *do*; question: *what kind*; object pronouns; modal verb *would*; verb + *to* + verb
REVIEW OF UNITS 1–4 — PAGES 26–27		
UNIT 5 — PAGES 28–33		
Tell me about your family. Families and family life	Talking about families and family members; exchanging information about the present; describing family life	Present continuous yes/no and Wh-questions, statements, and short answers; determiners: *all, nearly all, most, many, a lot of, some, not many, a few,* and *few*
UNIT 6 — PAGES 34–39		
How often do you exercise? Sports and exercise; routines	Asking about and describing routines and exercise; talking about frequency; talking about abilities	Adverbs of frequency: *always, almost always, usually, often, sometimes, seldom, hardly ever, almost never, never*; questions with *how: how often, how much time, how long, how well, how good*; short answers
UNIT 7 — PAGES 40–45		
We had a great time! Free-time and weekend activities; vacations	Talking about past events; giving opinions about past experiences; talking about vacations	Past tense yes/no and Wh-questions, statements, and short answers with regular and irregular verbs; past tense of *be*
UNIT 8 — PAGES 46–51		
How do you like the neighborhood? Stores and places in a city; neighborhoods; houses and apartments	Asking about and describing locations of places; asking about and describing neighborhoods; asking about quantities	*There is/there are; one, any, some*; prepositions of place; questions: *how much* and *how many*; countable and uncountable nouns
REVIEW OF UNITS 5–8 — PAGES 52–53		

Unit Summaries are on pages S-2–S-9; the Appendix is located in the back of the book.

Listening/Pronunciation	Writing/Reading	Interchange Activity
Recognizing formal and informal names; listening for personal information Intonation of clarification questions	Writing questions requesting personal information "Meeting and Greeting Customs": Reading about greeting customs	"Getting to know you": Collecting personal information from classmates
Listening to descriptions of jobs and daily schedules Unstressed words	Writing a description of an occupation "The Daily Grind": Reading about students with part-time work	"Common ground": Finding similarities in classmates' daily schedules
Listening to people shopping; listening for items, prices, and opinions Linked sounds	Writing a comparison of prices in different countries "Shop Till You Drop": Reading about different kinds of shopping	"Swap meet": Buying and selling things
Identifying musical styles; listening for likes and dislikes; listening to invitations Question intonation	Writing invitations and excuses "The Sound of Music": Reading about musicians from around the world	"What an invitation! What an excuse!": Making up unusual invitations and excuses
Listening for family relationships; listening to information about families and family life Blending with *does*	Writing a description of family life "The Changing Family": Reading about an American family	"Family facts": Finding out information about classmates' families and family members
Listening to people talk about free-time activities; listening to routines; listening to descriptions of sports participation Sentence stress	Writing a description of favorite activities "Smart Moves": Reading about fitness for the brain	"Fitness quiz": Interviewing about fitness habits
Listening to descriptions and opinions of past events and vacations Reduced forms of *did you*	Writing a postcard "Vacation Postcards": Reading about different kinds of vacations	"Vacation photos": Telling a story using pictures
Listening for locations of places; listening to descriptions of places in neighborhoods Reduced forms of *there is* and *there are*	Writing a description of a home "City Scenes": Reading about neighborhood life in cities around the world	"Neighborhood survey": Comparing two neighborhoods

1 Please call me Chuck.

1 CONVERSATION *Introducing yourself*

🔊 Listen and practice.

Elizabeth: Hello, I'm Elizabeth Mandel.
Chuck: Hi! My name is Charles Chang.
But please call me Chuck.
Elizabeth: Nice to meet you, Chuck.
You can call me Liz.
Chuck: OK. And what's your last
name again?
Elizabeth: Mandel.

2 CHECKING INFORMATION

A 🔊 Match the questions in column A with the responses in column B.
Listen and check. Then practice with a partner. Give your own information.

A

1. How do you pronounce your last name? ....
2. Excuse me, what's your first name again? ....
3. How do you spell your last name? ....
4. What do people call you? ....

B

a. C-H-A-N-G.
b. It's Mandel, with the accent on "del."
c. Well, everyone calls me Chuck.
d. Oh, it's Amy.

B *Group work* Make a list of names and nicknames for your group.
Introduce yourself with your full name. Use the expressions above.

A: Hi! I'm Joseph Block. Please call me Joe.
B: OK, Joe. And what's your last name again?
A: It's Block.

3 NAMES AND TITLES

A Use a title with a last name to address someone formally.

Titles	Single	Married
males: Mr.	✓	✓
females: Ms.	✓	✓
Miss	✓	
Mrs.		✓

Use a first name or nickname without a title to address someone informally.

B Listen to people talk to Chuck Chang, Elizabeth Mandel, and Amy Kim. Do they address them formally (**F**) or informally (**I**)?

1. ....   2. ....   3. ....   4. ....   5. ....   6. ....

4 CONVERSATION *Introducing someone*

A Listen and practice.

Tom: Paulo, who is that over there?
Paulo: Oh, that's my father! And that's my mother with him.
Tom: I'd like to meet them.

Paulo: Mom and Dad, this is Tom Hayes. Tom, these are my parents.
Tom: Pleased to meet you, Mr. and Mrs. Tavares.
Mrs. Tavares: Nice to meet you, Tom.
Paulo: My parents are here from Brazil. They're on vacation. 假期
Tom: Oh, where are you from in Brazil?
Mr. Tavares: We're from Rio.

B *Group work* Take turns introducing a partner to others.

A: Juan, this is Maria. She's from Argentina.
B: Hi, Maria.

3

5 GRAMMAR FOCUS

Wh-questions and statements with be

		Contractions		Subject pronouns	Possessive adjectives
What's your name?	My name **is** Chuck.	I am	= I'm	I	my
Where are you from?	I'm from Taiwan.	You are	= You're	you	your
		He is	= He's	he	his
Who is that?	His name **is** Tom.	She is	= She's	she	her
What's her name?	Her name **is** Amy.	It is	= It's	it	its
Where is she from?	She's from Korea.	We are	= We're	we	our
		They are	= They're	you	your
Where are you from?	We're from the United States.			they	their
		What is	= What's		
Who are they?	They're Amy's parents.				
What are their names?	Their names **are** Mr. and Mrs. Kim.				
Where are they from?	They're from Korea.				

For a list of countries and nationalities, see the appendix at the back of the book.

A Complete this conversation. Then compare with a partner.

Yoko: Rich, who are the two women
　　　over there?
Rich: Oh, ... names are Lisa
　　　and Kate.

Rich: Hi, Kate. This .... Yoko.
　　　.......... from Japan.
Yoko: Hello. Nice to meet you.
Kate: Good to meet you, Yoko.
Lisa: And .... name .... Lisa.
Yoko: Hi, Lisa.
Rich: Lisa and Kate .... from Canada.
Yoko: Oh? Where .... you from in Canada?
Kate: .... from Toronto.

B Complete these questions.
Then practice with a partner.

1. A: *Who   is*........ that?
　 B: That's Rich.

2. A: .... he from?
　 B: He's from Los Angeles.

3. A: .... his last name?
　 B: It's Brown.

4. A: .... the two students over there?
　 B: Their names are Lisa and Kate.

5. A: .... they from?
　 B: They're from Canada.

C *Group work* Write five questions about your classmates.
Then take turns asking and answering your questions.

Who is she?
Where is Su Hee from?

6 *SNAPSHOT*

Greetings from Around the World

a handshake 握手

a bow 鞠躬

a kiss on the cheek 面颊

a hug 拥抱

a pat on the back 轻拍

Source: Brigham Young University,
Center for International Studies

Talk about these questions.

Which greetings are typical in your country?
Can you name a country for each greeting?

7 *CONVERSATION* *Asking about someone*

A Listen and practice.

Sarah: Hi, Tom. How's everything?
  Tom: Not bad. How are you?
Sarah: Pretty good, thanks.

  Tom: Sarah, this is Paulo. He's from Brazil.
Sarah: Hello, Paulo. Are you on vacation?
Paulo: No, I'm not. I'm a student here.
Sarah: Oh, are you studying English?
Paulo: Well, yes, I am. And engineering, too.
Sarah: Are you and Tom in the same class?
Paulo: No, we aren't. But we're on the same
       volleyball team.

 CLASS AUDIO ONLY

B Listen to the rest of the conversation.

Where is Sarah from?

8 GRAMMAR FOCUS

Yes/No questions and short answers with be

Are you on vacation?	No, **I'm not**. **I'm** a student.
Are you a student?	Yes, **I am**.
Is Sarah from the United States?	No, she **isn't**. (No, she**'s not**.) She**'s** from Australia.
Is Sarah from Australia?	Yes, she **is**.
Are you and Tom in the same class?	No, we **aren't**. (No, we**'re not**.) We**'re** on the same volleyball team.
Are you and Tom on the volleyball team?	Yes, we **are**.
Are Mr. and Mrs. Tavares American?	No, they **aren't**. (No, they**'re not**.) They**'re** Brazilian.
Are Mr. and Mrs. Tavares Brazilian?	Yes, they **are**.

A Complete these conversations. Then practice with a partner.

1. A: .... you from the United States?
   B: Yes, I .... from Chicago.

2. A: .... Rosa in English 101?
   B: No, she .... in English 102.

3. A: .... you and Monique from France?
   B: Yes, we .... from Paris.

B *Pair work* Read the conversations in Exercises 4 and 7 again. Then answer these questions. For questions you answer "no," give the correct information.

1. Are Tom and Paulo on the baseball team? ....
2. Are Mr. and Mrs. Tavares on vacation? ....
3. Are Mr. and Mrs. Tavares from Mexico? ....
4. Is Paulo from Brazil? ....
5. Is Paulo on vacation? ....

C *Group work* Write five questions about your classmates. Then take turns asking and answering your questions.

> *Are Maria and Su Hee friends?*

interchange 1

Getting to know you
Find out about your classmates. Turn to page IC-2.

9 LISTENING

   Listen to these conversations and complete the information about each person.

First name	Last name	Where from?	Studying?
1. *Joe*		*the United States*	
2.	*Vera*		*engineering*
3. *Min Ho*	*Kim*		

10 *READING*

Meeting and Greeting Customs

How do you think the people in these countries greet each other?

There are many different greeting customs around the world. Here are some.

 Chile

People usually shake hands when they meet for the first time. When two women first meet, they sometimes give one kiss on the cheek. (They actually "kiss the air.") Women also greet both male and female friends with a kiss. Chilean men give their friends warm *abrazos* (hugs) or sometimes kiss women on the cheek.

 Finland

Finns greet each other with a firm handshake. Hugs and kisses are only for close friends and family.

 The Philippines

The everyday greeting for friends is a handshake for both men and women. Men sometimes pat each other on the back.

 Korea

Men bow slightly and shake hands to greet each other. Women do not usually shake hands. To address someone with his or her full name, the family name comes first, then the first name.

 The United States

People shake hands when they are first introduced. Friends and family members often hug or kiss on the cheek when they see each other. In these situations, men often kiss women but not other men.

A According to the article, in which country or countries are the following true? Check (✓) the correct boxes.

	Chile	Finland	the Philippines	Korea	the U.S.
1. People shake hands every time they meet.	☐	☐	☐	☐	☐
2. Women do not shake hands.	☐	☐	☐	☐	☐
3. Women kiss at the first meeting.	☐	☐	☐	☐	☐
4. Men hug or pat each other on the back.	☐	☐	☐	☐	☐
5. Women kiss male friends.	☐	☐	☐	☐	☐
6. The family name comes first.	☐	☐	☐	☐	☐

B *Pair work* How do these people greet each other in your country?

1. two male friends
2. a male and female friend
3. two strangers
4. two female friends

2 How do you spend your day?

1 SNAPSHOT

Work and School Days

	Brazil	the United Kingdom	South Korea	the United States
Average number of working hours per week	44	44	48	40
Average number of paid vacation days per year	20–21	27	20	12
Number of national holidays	10	8	10	11
Number of school days per year	182	192	222	178
Hours of instruction in school per day	4.5	5	4.5	5.5

Information compiled from *The New York Times,*
Digest of Educational Statistics, and interviews.

Talk about these questions.

Which country would you like to work in? Why?
Where would you like to be a student? Why?

2 WORD POWER Jobs

A Complete the word map with jobs from the list.

architect
receptionist
company director
flight attendant
supervisor 领导人，监察人
engineer
salesperson
secretary
professor
sales manager
security guard
word processor
加工者，分程者

Professionals
architect
professor
engineer
doctor
lawyer

Service occupations
flight attendant
salesperson
secretary
receptionist
security guard

Jobs

Management positions
company director
supervisor
sales manager

Office work
receptionist
secretary
word processor

B Add two more jobs to each category. Then compare with a partner.

3 WORK AND WORKPLACES

A Look at the pictures. Match the information in columns A, B, and C.

A	B	C
a salesperson	for an airline	builds houses
a chef	in a restaurant	cares for patients
a flight attendant	for a construction company	answers the phone
a carpenter	in a hospital	cooks food
a receptionist	in a department store	serves passengers 乘客 旅客
a nurse	in an office	sells clothes

interpreter 翻譯
astronomer

B *Pair work* Take turns describing each person's job.

"She's a salesperson. She works in a department store. She sells clothes."

4 CONVERSATION *Describing work*

A Listen and practice.

Jason: Where do you work, Andrea?
Andrea: I work for Thomas Cook Travel.
Jason: Oh, really? What do you do there?
Andrea: I'm a guide. I take people on tours to countries in South America, like Peru.
Jason: That sounds interesting!
Andrea: Yes, it's a great job. I love it. And what do you do?
Jason: I'm a student, and I have a part-time job, too.
Andrea: Oh? Where do you work?
Jason: In a fast-food restaurant.
Andrea: Which restaurant?
Jason: Hamburger Heaven.

CLASS AUDIO ONLY ▶ **B** Listen to the rest of the conversation.

1. What does Jason do, exactly?
2. How does he like his job?

5 GRAMMAR FOCUS

Simple present Wh-questions and statements

What do you **do**?	**I'm** a student, and **I have** a part-time job.	**I/You**	**He/She**
Where do you **work**?	**I work** at/in a restaurant.	work	works
Where do you **go** to school?	**I go** to the University of Texas.	take	takes
How do you **like** your school?	**I like** it very much.	study	studies
		teach	teaches
Where does Andrea **work**?	She **works** for Thomas Cook Travel.	do	does
What does she **do**?	She's a guide. She **takes** people on tours.	go	goes
Where does Jason **go** to school?	He **goes** to New York University.	have	has
How does he **like** it?	He **loves** it.		

A Complete these conversations. Then practice with a partner.

1. A: What _do_ you _do_?
   B: I'm a student. I study business.
   A: And _where_ do you _go_ to school?
   B: I _go_ to Jefferson College.
   A: _How_ do you like your classes?
   B: I _like_ them a lot.

2. A: What _does_ Kanya do?
   B: She's a teacher. She _is_ mathematics
      at a school in Bangkok.
   A: And what about Somsak? Where _does_ he work?
   B: He _works_ for an electronics company.
   A: _What_ does he do, exactly?
   B: He's a salesman. He _sales_ computer equipment.

B *Pair work* What do you know about these jobs? Complete the chart.
Then write sentences describing each job, using *he* or *she*.

A doctor	A travel agent	A police officer
▪ works in a hospital	▪	▪ ....
▪ has an office	▪	▪ ....
▪ works long hours	▪	▪ ....
▪ cares for patients	▪	▪ ....

> A doctor works in a hospital. She has an office, too. . . .

C *Group work* Ask your classmates questions about work and school.

A: What do you do, Aki?
B: I'm a student.
C: Where do you go to school?
B: . . .

6 *WRITING*

A Write a description of what you do. Don't write your name on the paper.

> *I'm a student. I go to McGill University in Canada.*
> *I'm a freshman. I study computer science. I work*
> *part time at a radio station, too. I'm a disc jockey.*
> *I play music. I love my job!*

B *Group work* Pass your descriptions around the group. Can you guess who wrote each description?

7 *CONVERSATION* *Daily schedules*

A Listen and practice.

Daniel: How do you spend your day, Helen?
Helen: Well, on weekdays I get up around ten. Then I read the paper for an hour and have lunch at about noon.
Daniel: Really? What time do you go to work?
Helen: I start work at three.
Daniel: And when do you get home at night?
Helen: I get home pretty late, around midnight.
Daniel: So what do you do, exactly?
Helen: I'm a TV announcer. Don't you recognize me? I do the weather report on KNTV!
Daniel: Gee, I'm sorry. I don't watch TV.

CLASS AUDIO ONLY ▶ **B** Listen to Daniel describe how he spends his day.

1. What time does he get up? start work? study until?
2. What does he do?

8 *PRONUNCIATION* *Unstressed words*

A Listen and practice. The prepositions in these sentences (*around, for,* and *at*) are not stressed.

I get **úp** around **tén.**
I read the **pá**per for an **hóur.**
I have **lúnch** at about **nóon.**

B *Pair work* Practice the conversation in Exercise 7 again. Be careful not to stress prepositions.

9 GRAMMAR FOCUS

Time expressions 🔊

I get up	**at** 7:00	**in** the morning	**on** weekdays.
I go to bed	**around** ten	**in** the evening	**on** weeknights.
I leave work	**early**	**in** the afternoon	**on** weekends.
I get home	**late**	**at** night	**on** Fridays.
I stay up	**until** midnight	**on** Saturdays.	
I wake up	**before/after** noon	**on** Sundays.	

Ways to express clock time
7:00
seven o'clock
seven
7:00 in the morning = 7:00 A.M.
7:00 in the evening = 7:00 P.M.

A Complete these sentences with time expressions.

1. I get up ....*at*...... six ...*in*... the morning
   ...*on*.... weekdays.
2. I go to bed .....*at*...... midnight ...*on*... weeknights.
3. I start work .....*at*...... 11:30 ...*on*... night.
4. I arrive at work ....*on*.......... Mondays,
   .....*at*.... 7:00 A.M.
5. I have lunch ......*at*....... three ...*in*.... the afternoon
   ...*on*.... weekdays.
6. I stay up ....*on*.......... weekends.
7. I have a little snack ....*at*..... 9:00 ...*in*.... the evening.
8. I sleep ......*until*..... noon ...*on*..... Sundays.

B Rewrite the sentences above so that they are true for you.
Then compare with a partner.

C *Pair work* Take turns asking and answering these questions.

1. What days do you get up early? late?
2. What are two things you do before 8:00 in the morning?
3. What are three things you do on Saturday mornings?
4. How late do you stay up on Saturday nights?
5. What is something you do only on Sundays?

interchange 2

Common ground
Take a survey. Compare
your schedule with your
classmates' schedules.
Turn to page IC-3.

10 LISTENING

CLASS AUDIO ONLY ▶ **A** 🔊 Listen to Rodney, Tina, and Ellen talk about
their daily schedules. Complete the chart.

	Job	Gets up at . . .	Gets home at . . .	Goes to bed at . . .
Rodney	*chef*			
Tina	*office manager*			
Ellen	*flight attendant*			

B *Class activity* Who do you think has the best daily schedule? Why?

11 READING

The Daily Grind

Is it a good idea for a student to have a job? Why or why not?

Brandon Smith

I'm a junior in high school, and I have a part-time job in a restaurant. I bus dishes on Saturdays and Sundays from 8:00 until 4:00. I earn $5.50 an hour. It isn't much money, but I save almost every penny! I want to go to a good university, and the cost goes up every year. Of course, I spend some money when I go out on Saturday nights.

Lauren Russell

I'm a senior in high school. I have a job as a cashier in a grocery store. The job pays well – about $6.75 an hour. I work every weeknight after school from 4:00 until 8:00. I don't have time for homework, and my grades aren't very good this year. But I have to work, or I can't buy nice clothes and I can't go out on Saturday nights. Also, a car costs a lot of money.

Erica Davis

I'm a freshman in college. College is very expensive, so I work in a law office for three hours every weekday afternoon. I make photocopies, file papers, and sort mail for $8.25 an hour. The job gives me good experience because I want to be a lawyer someday. But I don't want to work every semester. I need time to study.

A Read the article. Why do these students work? Check (✓) the correct boxes.

	Brandon	Lauren	Erica
1. To earn money for college	☐	☐	☐
2. To buy nice clothes	☐	☐	☐
3. To go out on the weekend	☐	☐	☐
4. To pay for a car	☐	☐	☐
5. To get job experience	☐	☐	☐

B *Pair work* Talk about these questions.

1. Look at the reasons why each student works. Who has good reasons to work? Who doesn't, in your opinion?
2. How many hours a week does each student work?
3. How much money does each student earn per week?
4. What are the advantages and disadvantages of part-time work for students?

3 How much is it?

1 SNAPSHOT

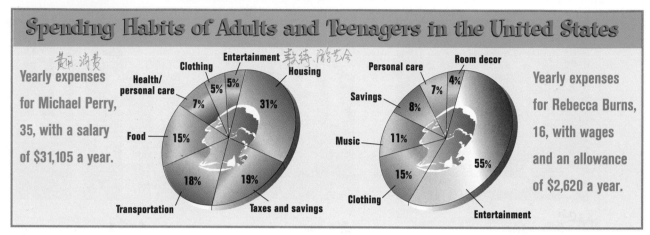

Spending Habits of Adults and Teenagers in the United States

Yearly expenses for Michael Perry, 35, with a salary of $31,105 a year.

Entertainment
Clothing 5%
5%
Health/personal care 7%
Housing 31%
Food 15%
Transportation 18%
Taxes and savings 19%

Yearly expenses for Rebecca Burns, 16, with wages and an allowance of $2,620 a year.

Personal care
Room decor 4%
7%
Savings 8%
Music 11%
Entertainment 55%
Clothing 15%

Portraits based on information from the *Statistical Abstract of the U.S.* and the Rand Youth Poll.

Talk about these questions.

How does Michael Perry spend most of his money?
How does Rebecca Burns spend most of her money?
How do their spending habits compare?
How do you spend your money? Make two lists: things you have to buy and things you like to buy.

2 CONVERSATION Prices

A Listen and practice.

Steve: Oh, look at those earrings, Maria. They're perfect for you.
Maria: These red ones? I'm not sure.
Steve: No, the yellow ones.
Maria: Oh, these? Hmm. Yellow isn't a good color for me.
Steve: Well, that necklace isn't bad.
Maria: Which one?
Steve: That blue one right there. How much is it?
Maria: It's $42! That's expensive!
Steve: Hey, let me get it for you. It's your birthday present.

CLASS AUDIO ONLY ▶ **B** Listen to the rest of the conversation.

1. What else do they buy?
2. Who pays for it?

$24"
$36"
$42"
$22"
$18"
$26"

14

3 GRAMMAR FOCUS

Demonstratives; one, ones

How much is **this** necklace? **this one**? How much are **these** earrings? **these**?	How much is **that** necklace? **that one**? How much are **those** earrings? **those**?	Which **one**? The blue **one**. It's $42. Which **ones**? The yellow **ones**. They're $18.

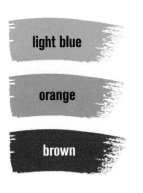

Prices
$42 = forty-two dollars
$59.95 = fifty-nine ninety-five **or** fifty-nine dollars and ninety-five cents

Colors

gole silver beige ciyan oline navy

light blue	dark blue	green	yellow
orange	pink	red	purple
brown	black	gray	white

Look at the pictures and complete these conversations.
Then practice with a partner.

1. A: Excuse me. How much
   ...*are these*... jeans?
   B: Which ...*ones*...? Do you mean ...*these*...?
   A: No, the light blue ...*one*... .
   B: Oh, ...*it's*... $59.95.
   A: Almost sixty dollars! Are you kidding?

2. A: I like ...*the*... backpack over there.
   How much ...*is*... it?
   B: Which ...*one*...? Each backpack has a
   different price.
   A: ...*The*... red ...*one*... .
   B: It's $98.50. But ...*the*... green
   ...*one*... is only $45.
   A: OK. Let me look at it.

4 THAT'S EXPENSIVE!

Pair work Ask and answer questions about these products.
For help with numbers, see the appendix at the back of the book.

A: How much is the computer?
B: Which one?
A: The small one./This one.
B: It's $5,456.
A: That's expensive!

useful expressions
That's cheap.
That's reasonable.
That's OK/not bad.
That's expensive.

5 LISTENING

   Listen to Tim and Sandra shopping, and complete the chart.

Item	Price	Do they buy it?		Reason
		Yes	No	
1. Rollerblades	165	☐	☑	expensive
2. cap	99.5	☑	☐	
3. sunglasses	16	☐	☑	too big. too expensive

6 PRONUNCIATION *Linked sounds*

A Listen and practice. Final consonants are often linked to the vowels that follow them.

A: How much are these pants?
B: They're forty-eight dollars.

A: And how much is this sweater?
B: It's thirty-seven dollars.

B *Pair work* Ask and answer four questions about prices in this unit. Pay attention to the linked sounds.

Swap meet
See what kinds of deals you can make as a buyer and a seller. Turn to pages IC-4 and IC-5.

7 WORD POWER Materials

A *Pair work* Identify these things. Use the words from the list.
What other materials are these things sometimes made of? Make a list.

a **cotton** shirt   **leather** gloves   a **plastic** bracelet   a **silk** scarf
a **gold** ring   **polyester** pants   **rubber** boots   **silver** earrings

1. *a plastic bracelet*   2. *a gold ring*   3. *a silk scarf*   4. *polyester pants*

5. *leather gloves*   6. *a cotton shirt*   7. *silver earrings*   8. *rubber boots*

B *Class activity* Which of the materials can you find in your classroom?

"Juan has a leather bag."

8 CONVERSATION Shopping

A 🔊 Listen and practice.

Anne: Look! These jackets are nice.
        Which one do you like better?
  Sue: I like the wool one better.
Anne: Really? Why?
  Sue: It looks warmer.
Anne: Well, I prefer the leather one.
        It's more attractive than the wool one.
  Sue: Hmm. There's no price tag.
Anne: Excuse me. How much is this jacket?
Clerk: It's $499. Would you like to try it on?
Anne: Oh, no. That's OK! But thank you anyway.
Clerk: You're welcome.

B 🔊 Listen to the rest of the conversation.

1. What does Anne buy?
2. What does Sue think of it?

9 GRAMMAR FOCUS

big + er than

Preferences; comparisons with adjectives 🔊

Which one do you **prefer**? I **prefer** the leather one. Which one do you **like better/more**? I **like** the leather one **better/more**.	That one is **nicer than** the wool one. This one is **cheaper than** . . . . The leather jacket is **prettier than** . . . . It looks **bigger than** . . . . It's **more attractive than**	nice → nicer cheap → cheap**er** pretty → prett**ier** big → big**ger** good → **better**

For more information on comparatives, see the appendix at the back of the book.

A Complete these conversations. Then practice with a partner.

  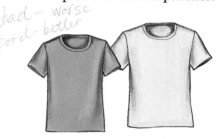 

bad – worse
good – better

polyester tie   silk tie   medium shirt   large shirt   leather boots   rubber boots

1. A: Which tie is *prettier*, the orange one or the blue one? (pretty)
   B: Well, the blue one is silk. And silk is *nicer than* polyester. (nice)

2. A: Is this green shirt *larger than* that yellow one? (large)
   B: No, the yellow one is *bigger*. It's a large. The green one is a medium. (big)

3. A: Which are *cheaper*, the brown boots or the black ones? (cheap)
   B: The brown ones are leather. And leather is *more expensive than* rubber. (expensive)

B *Pair work* Compare the items above with a partner. Give your own opinions.

A: Which tie do you like better?
B: I like the orange one better. The design is nicer.

useful expressions

The color is prettier.
The design is nicer.
The style is more attractive.
The material is better.

10 WRITING

How much do these items cost in your country? Fill in the chart.
Then compare the prices in your country with the prices in the U.S.

	Cost in my country	Cost in the U.S.
gasoline汽油	....	$ 1.10/gallon
a compact disc	....	$ 12.99
a haircut	....	$ 23.00
a pair of jeans	....	$ 34.00

Many things are more expensive in my country than in the United States. For example, a liter of gas is about $.66. In the U.S. it's cheaper. It's about $1.10 per gallon. . . .

11 *READING*

Shop Till You Drop

Look at the pictures of different kinds of shopping in the United States.
What kind of shopping can you do in your country?

Catalog Shopping

People in the United States often shop from catalogs. There are special catalogs for almost every need – including clothing, furniture, health and beauty products, and things for the kitchen. People also order about 40% of their music from music club catalogs. Customers say that music stores are too noisy.

Television Shopping

Television shopping began in 1986. About 5% to 8% of the American public now shops by television. Some popular shopping channels are the Home Shopping Network and QVC. Customers say that television shopping is easier than shopping in a store. How do they buy things? They make a phone call and charge the item to their credit card. And TV shopping channels are on late at night, so people can "go shopping" anytime.

Computer Shopping

Is computer shopping the way of the future? About 37% of American households now have personal computers. And shopping by computer (or "shopping on-line") is interesting to more people every day. Already, shoppers can use their computers to order many different products, such as computer products, flowers, food, T-shirts, and posters. And new on-line shopping services appear every day. Soon people may be able to shop for anything, anytime, anywhere in the world.

A Read the article. Check (✓) True or False. For the false statements, give the correct information.

	True	False
1. About 60% of music in the United States is sold through music stores.	☐	☐
2. The Home Shopping Network is the name of a computer shopping service.	☐	☐
3. About 37% of American households do their shopping through the computer.	☐	☐

B *Pair work* Talk about these questions.

1. Do you like shopping? How often do you usually shop?
2. What kinds of shopping do you like? Check (✓) the appropriate boxes.

☐ shopping at discount stores
☐ television shopping
☐ shopping at department stores

☐ shopping at small stores
☐ catalog shopping
☐ shopping at secondhand or thrift stores

☐ computer shopping
☐ shopping at a mall

4 Do you like jazz?

couleurs jazz

1 SNAPSHOT

Music Sales in the United States

Other 8%
Gospel 3%
Jazz 3%
Classical 4%
Pop 13%
Country 18%
Rock 33%
Rap/Urban 18%

Source: The Recording Industry Association of America

Talk about these questions.

Which of these kinds of music do people in your country listen to?
What other kinds of music do people in your country like?

CLASS AUDIO ONLY ▶ *Listen and number the musical styles from 1 to 8 as you hear them.*

...3... classical   ...2... gospel   ...8... New Age   ...5... rap
...6... country   ...4... jazz   ...1... pop   ...7... rock

2 WORD POWER Entertainment

A Complete the chart with words from the list. *love/Romance documentay. drama historical musical action*

classical   salsa   *suspense war*
game shows   science fiction   *cartoons*
horror films   soap operas 爬虫劇 *copic*
jazz   talk shows
news   thrillers 恐强
pop   westerns 西部片

B Add three more words to each category. Then compare with a partner.

C Number the items in each list from 1 (you like it the most) to 7 (you like it the least).

Entertainment

TV programs
game shows
news
talk shows
soap operas

Movies
horror films
science fiction
thrillers
westerns

Music
classical
jazz
pop
salsa

3 CONVERSATION *Likes and dislikes*

A Listen and practice.

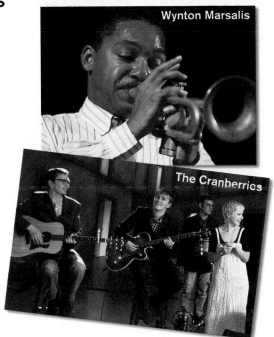
Wynton Marsalis

The Cranberries

Liz: Do you like jazz, Tom?
Tom: No, I don't like it very much. Do you?
Liz: Well, yes, I do. I'm a real fan of
     Wynton Marsalis.
Tom: Oh, does he play the piano?
Liz: No, he doesn't! He plays the trumpet.
     So, what kind of music do you like?
Tom: I like rock a lot.
Liz: Who's your favorite group?
Tom: The Cranberries. I love their music.
     How about you? Do you like them?
Liz: No, I don't. I can't stand them!

CLASS AUDIO ONLY ▶ **B** Listen to the rest of the conversation.

1. Who is Liz's favorite singer?
2. Does Tom like that singer? Why or why not?

4 GRAMMAR FOCUS

Yes/No and Wh-questions with do

		Object pronouns
Do you **like** jazz?	**What kind of** music **do** you **like**?	me
Yes, **I do**. I like it a lot.	I like rock a lot.	you (singular)
No, **I don't** like it very much.		him
		her
Does he **play** the piano?	**What does** he **play**?	it
Yes, he **does**.	He plays the trumpet.	us
No, he **doesn't**.		you (plural)
		them
Do they **like** The Cranberries?	**Who do** they **like**?	
Yes, they **do**. They love them.	They like R.E.M.	
No, they **don't** like them very much.		

Complete these conversations. Then practice with a partner.

1. A: ...*Do*... you like horror films?
   B: No, I ...*don't*... like ...*them*... very much. I like comedies.
   A: How about Lisa and Brian? ...*Do*... they like horror films?
   B: Well, I think Brian ...*does*... Why don't you ask ...*him*...?

2. A: ...*Do*... you like the singer Bonnie Raitt?
   B: Yes, I ...*do*... I really like ...*her*... a lot.
   A: What ...*kind*... of music ...*does*... she sing?
   B: She's a rock singer.
   A: ...*Does*... she sing country music, too?
   B: I don't know. I have her new CD. Let's listen to ...*it*...

5 PRONUNCIATION Question intonation

A 🎧 Listen and practice. Yes/No questions usually have rising intonation. Wh-questions usually have falling intonation.

Do you like movies?   What kind of movies do you like?

Do you like pop music?   What kind of music do you like?

B Practice these questions.

Do you like TV?   What programs do you like?
Do you like music videos?   What videos do you like?

6 ENTERTAINMENT SURVEY

A *Group work* Write five questions about entertainment and entertainers. Then ask and answer your questions in groups.

Do you like . . . ?
   (pop music, TV, movies, plays)
What kinds of . . . do you like?
   (music, movies, TV programs)
What do you think of . . . ?
   (*Star Trek*, horror films,
   gospel music)

Gloria Estefan

Brad Pitt

Patrick Stewart

B *Group work* Complete this information about your group.

Our Group Favorites	
What's your favorite kind of . . . ?	**Who's your favorite . . . ?**
music:	singer: ....
movie:	actor: ....
TV program:	actress: ....

C *Class activity* Read your group's list to the class. Then find out the class favorites.

useful expressions

Our favorite . . . is . . . .
We all like . . . .
We don't agree on . . . .
We can't stand . . . .

7 *LISTENING* TV game show

A Listen to four people playing *Who's My Date?* Three men want to invite Linda on a date. What kinds of things do they like? What kinds of things does Linda like?

	Music	**Movies**	**TV programs**
Bill	classical	horror film thrillers news	
John	Jazz	westerns	talk shows
Tony	rock	horror	game shows
Linda	pop	horror	TV game show talk shows

B *Class activity* Who do you think is the best date for Linda?

8 *CONVERSATION* Invitations

Listen and practice.

Dave: I have tickets to *The Phantom of the Opera* on Friday night. Would you like to go?
Susan: Thanks. I'd love to. What time is the show?
Dave: It's at 8:00.
Susan: That sounds great. So, do you want to have dinner at 6:00?
Dave: Uh, I'd like to, but I have to work late.
Susan: Oh, that's OK. Let's just meet at the theater before the show, around 7:30.
Dave: That sounds fine.

a scene from *The Phantom of the Opera*

9 GRAMMAR FOCUS

Would; *verb* + to + *verb*

Would you **like to go** out on Saturday night? Yes, I **would**. Yes, I'd **love to**. Thanks. Yes, I'd really **like to go**.	**Would** you **like to see** a movie? I'd **like to**, but I **have to work** late. I'd **like to**, but I **need to save** money. I'd **like to**, but I **want to visit** my parents.	***Contraction*** I would = I'd

I'm looking foraway to it.

A Respond to these invitations. Then practice with a partner.

1. A: I have tickets to the baseball game on Saturday. Would you like to go?
   B: ....

2. A: Would you like to come over for dinner tonight?
   B: ....

3. A: Would you like to go to the gym with me on Friday night?
   B: ....

4. A: There's a great movie on TV tonight. Would you like to watch it with me?
   B: ....

B *Pair work* Think of three different things you would like to do. Then invite
a partner to do them with you. Ask and answer follow-up questions like these:

When is it?   What time does it start?
Where is it?   What time should I/we . . . ?

10 LISTENING

Listen to three people inviting friends to events and activities.
Complete the chart. Do the friends accept the invitations?

	Event/Activity	Day	Time	Accept?	
				Yes	**No**
1. Jake and Paula	movie	3	9:00	☐	☑
2. Lucy and Chris	Jazz	4	8:30	☑	☐
3. Rich and Ed	baseball	5	2:00 PM	☑	☐

11 WRITING

See Interchange 4 for the writing assignment.

interchange 4

**What an invitation!
What an excuse!**

Make up unusual
invitations and funny
excuses. Turn to
page IC-6.

12 *READING*

The Sound of Music

What are some traditional kinds of music in your country?

Do you like popular music from Latin America, the United States, or Asia? Many musicians from around the world blend their country's music with popular sounds.

Caetano Veloso

After thirty years, Caetano Veloso is still one of Brazil's most important musicians. He mixes rock with the music of the Bahia region. Bahia is a state of Brazil that is strongly influenced by African culture. Caetano Veloso is an excellent songwriter and poet. He says of his music, "I make my records like a painter paints his canvas."

Bonnie Raitt

Bonnie Raitt is an American singer, songwriter, and guitarist. Her music blends rock with country and the blues. The blues is a kind of folk music that is often sad. It is usually about love and the problems of life. Bonnie Raitt's strong, rough voice is perfect for singing country and the blues.

Cui Jian

Cui Jian [pronounced "tsay jyan"] is a very important musician in the growth of rock music in China. Western styles, like jazz and rap, clearly influence his music. However, his music is very Chinese in its instruments and sounds. Cui Jian says his music expresses the feelings of Chinese young people.

A Read about the three musicians. Complete the chart.

	Nationality	Types of music he/she blends
1. Caetano Veloso	....	....
2. Bonnie Raitt	....	....
3. Cui Jian	....	....

B *Pair work* Talk about these questions.

1. What do these three musicians have in common?
2. How does Caetano Veloso make his records?
3. Why is Bonnie Raitt's voice good for country and blues music?
4. What does Cui Jian want his music to express?

1 GETTING TO KNOW YOU

Pair work You are talking to someone at school.
Have a conversation.

A: Hi. How are you?
B: . . .
A: By the way, my name is . . . .
B: How do you pronounce your name again?
A: . . . Where are you from?
B: . . .
A: Are you a student here?
B: . . . And how about you? What do you do?
A: . . .
B: Oh, really? And where are you from?
A: . . .
B: Well, nice talking to you. . . .

2 WHAT'S THE QUESTION?

Look at these answers. Write the questions.
Then compare with a partner.

1. No, Teresa and I aren't in the same class. She's in the morning class.

2. My sister? She goes to the University of Toronto.

3. I get up before 11:00 A.M. on Sundays.

4. No, my teacher isn't American. She's Canadian.

5. Rock music is OK, but I like jazz better.

6. I leave home at 6:30 in the evening on weekdays.

7. A video? Sure, I'd love to watch one with you.

8. The red sweater is nicer than the purple one.

3 **ROLE PLAY** *In a department store*

Pair work Put items "for sale" on your desk or a table –
notebooks, watches, or bags. Use items of different colors.

Student A: You are a clerk. Answer the customer's questions.

Student B: You are a customer. Ask about the price of each item.
Say if you want to buy it.

A: Can I help you?
B: Yes. I like that . . . . How much . . . ?
A: Which one(s)?
B: . . .

Change roles and try the role play again.

4 **LISTENING**

 Listen to people asking questions at a party. Check (✓) the best response.

1. ☐ I work in an office.
   ☐ Yes, very early. Before 7:00 A.M.

2. ☐ Not very much.
   ☐ Oh, I just stay in and work around the house.

3. ☐ Yes, I have a laptop.
   ☐ A good laptop computer costs over $2,000.

4. ☐ Yes, I'm from Italy.
   ☐ Actually, I work here.

5. ☐ Almost any kind except classical.
   ☐ No, I don't play the piano.

6. ☐ Thanks, I'd love to. What time?
   ☐ It's on at the Varsity Theater.

5 **TV AND RADIO**

A ***Pair work*** Take turns asking and
answering these questions.

TV

When do you usually watch TV?
What kinds of programs do you prefer?
What's your favorite channel?
What's your favorite program?
What time is it on?
Do you watch . . . (name of program)?

B ***Pair work*** Change partners. Take turns
asking and answering these questions.

Radio

When do you listen to the radio?
What kinds of programs do you listen to?
Do you listen to programs in English?

What's your favorite radio station?
Who are your favorite singers and groups?
What's your favorite radio program?

5 Tell me about your family.

1 WORD POWER The family

A Look at Sam's family tree. How are these people related to him?
Add these words to the family tree.

cousin
father
grandmother
niece
sister-in-law
uncle
wife

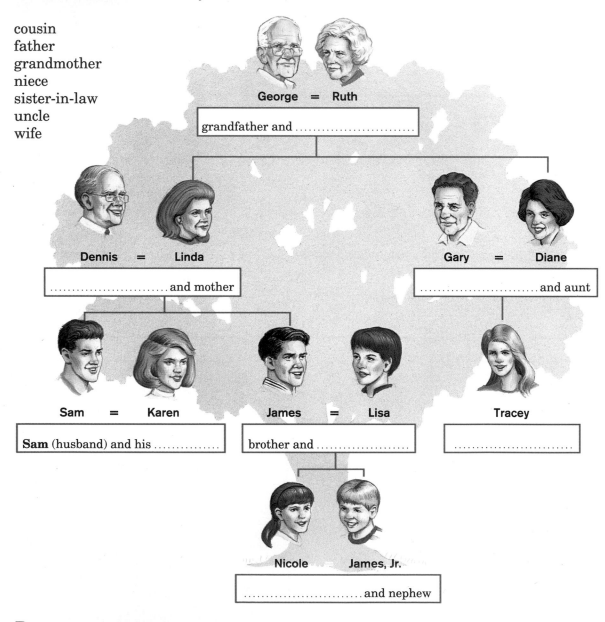

George = Ruth

grandfather and ....

Dennis = Linda

...........................and mother

Gary = Diane

...........................and aunt

Sam = Karen

Sam (husband) and his ....

James = Lisa

brother and ....

Tracey

....

Nicole   James, Jr.

...........................and nephew

B *Pair work* Draw your family tree. Then take turns talking about
your families. Ask follow-up questions to get more information.

For a single person:

There are 6 in my family.
I have 2 sisters and a brother.

For a married person:

There are 4 in my family.
We have a daughter and a son.

Follow-up questions:

Where do/does your . . . live?
What do/does your . . . do?

2 *LISTENING* Hollywood families

  Listen to two conversations about famous people. How are the people related?

1.
Warren
Beatty

Shirley
MacLaine

Annette
Bening

2.
Charlie
Sheen

Martin
Sheen

Emilio
Estevez

....

3 *CONVERSATION* Asking about families

A Listen and practice.

Rita: Tell me about your brother and sister, Sue.
Sue: Well, my sister is a lawyer.
Rita: Really? Does she live here in Seattle?
Sue: Yes, she does. But she's working in
      Washington, D.C., right now.
      Her job is top secret.
Rita: Wow! And what does your brother do?
Sue: He's a painter. He's working in Argentina
      this month. He has an exhibition there.
Rita: What an interesting family!

B Listen to the rest of the conversation.

1. Where do Rita's parents live?
2. What do they do?

4 *PRONUNCIATION* Blending with does

 Listen and practice. Notice the blending of **does** with other words.

1. A: My brother is married.
      [dəziy]
   B: **Does he** have any children?
   A: Yes, he does.
      [wədəziy]
   B: **What does he** do?
   A: He's a painter.

2. A: My sister lives in Seattle.
      [dəʃiy]
   B: **Does she** live with you?
   A: No, she doesn't.
      [wədəʃiy]
   B: **What does she** do?
   A: She's a lawyer.

5 GRAMMAR FOCUS

Present continuous

Are you **living** at home now?	Yes, I **am**./No, I**'m not**.	**Some verbs generally not used in the present continuous**
Is she still **working** in Seattle?	Yes, she **is**./No, she **isn't**.	have
Are they **going** to college this year?	Yes, they **are**./No, they **aren't**.	know
		like
Where **are** you **working** this month?	I**'m working** in Japan.	love
What **is** she **doing** these days?	She**'s teaching** at a university.	want
Who **are** they **visiting** this week?	They**'re visiting** their parents.	

A Complete these conversations using the present tense or the present continuous. Then practice with a partner.

1. A: Is anyone in your family looking for a job?
   B: Yes, my sister is. She _is working_ (work) part time in a restaurant now, but she _is looking_ (look) for a job in a theater company. She _loves_ (love) acting.

2. A: What is your brother doing these days?
   B: He _is going_ (go) to college this semester. He _likes_ (like) it a lot. He _is studing_ (study) mathematics.

3. A: Where do your parents live?
   B: They _live_ (live) in Chicago most of the time, but they _is staying_ (stay) in Florida this winter. They _have_ (have) a house there.

B *Pair work* Take turns asking the questions in part A or similar questions of your own. Give your own information when answering.

C *Group work* Take turns. Ask each student about his or her family. Then ask follow-up questions to get more information.

Topics to ask about
traveling
living abroad 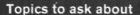
taking a class
moving to a new home
going to college or high school
studying a foreign language
looking for a job

A: Is anyone in your family traveling right now?
B: Yes, my father is.
C: Where is he?
B: He's in Bangkok.
D: What's he doing there?
B: . . .

Family facts
Find out some interesting facts about your classmates' families. Turn to page IC-7.

6 SNAPSHOT

Facts About Families in the United States

Children

57% of children under six have two parents who work or a single parent who works.

63% of women with children work.

50% of working women return to work within a year of having a baby.

Marriage

50% of marriages end in divorce.

80% of divorced people remarry; more than 50% divorce again.

Elderly

20% to 30% of the population now cares for an elderly relative, or will within five years.

Source: The Family and Medical Leave Act

Talk about these questions.

Which of these facts surprises you?
Do women with children usually work in your country?
Do people often get divorced?
Do elderly people generally live with relatives?

7 CONVERSATION Describing family life

A Listen and practice.

Ryan: Look at this headline, Soo Mi.
Soo Mi: Wow! So many people in the United States get divorced!
Ryan: Is it the same in Korea?
Soo Mi: I don't think so. In Korea, some marriages break up, but most couples stay together.
Ryan: Do people get married young?
Soo Mi: Not really. Very few people get married before the age of 20.
Ryan: Hmm. Do women usually work after they get married?
Soo Mi: No, a lot of women stay home and take care of their families. But some work.

B Listen to the rest of the conversation.

What does Ryan say about families in the United States? Write down two things.

8 GRAMMAR FOCUS

Determiners 📼

100%	All Nearly all Most	women with children work.
	Many A lot of Some	women stay home after they get married.
	Not many A few Few	couples stay together.
0%	No one	gets married before the age of 20.

Handwritten margin notes: 95% / 85-90 / 75-8 / 50-75 / 50-60 / 30 / 20 / 10

A Rewrite these sentences using determiners. Then compare with a partner.

1. In Australia, 87% of married couples have children.
   ...Most..

2. Six percent of 20- to 24-year-olds in the United States are divorced.
   ..Few...

3. Thirty-five percent of the people in Germany live alone.
   ..Not many...

4. In China, 50% of women get married by the age of 22.
   ..A lot of..
   many
   some

B *Pair work* Rewrite the sentences in part A so that they are about your country. Then discuss your information with a partner.

> *In my country, only some married couples have children.*

useful expressions

Is that right?
Do you think so? I think . . . .
I don't agree.
I don't think so.
It's different in my country.

9 WRITING

A Write about families in your country. Use some of your ideas from Exercise 8.

> *In my country, most people get married by the age of 30. Not many women work after they get married. Grandparents, parents, and children often live in the same house. . . .*

B *Group work* Take turns reading your compositions. Then answer any questions from the group.

10 READING

The Changing Family

What kinds of problems do parents have in your country?

Now that Judy is working, Steve has to help her more with the housework. He doesn't enjoy it, however.

Judy loves her work, but she feels tired and too busy. She also worries about the children. Judy has to work on Saturdays, so Steve and Judy don't have a lot of free time together.

American families are changing. One important change is that most married women now work outside the home. What happens when both parents work? Read about the Morales family.

Judy and Steve Morales have three children: Josh, 12; Ben, 9; and Emily, 6. Steve is a computer programmer. This year, Judy is working again as a hospital administrator. The family needs the money, and Judy likes her job. Everything is going well, but there are also some problems.

Emily is having a great time in her after-school program. When Judy comes to pick her up, she doesn't want to leave.

Unfortunately, Ben's school doesn't have an after-school program. Right now, he's spending most afternoons by himself in front of the TV.

Josh is enjoying his new freedom after school. He's playing his music louder and spending more time on the phone. He's also doing a few household chores.

A Read the article. What are Steve's and Judy's problems? Complete the chart.

Problems	
1. Steve	....
2. Judy	....
3. Steve and Judy	....

B *Pair work* Talk about these questions.

1. Which of the problems above do you think is the most serious?
   Offer some solutions for that problem.
2. Which of the children are benefiting from Judy's working?
   Which one is not?

6 How often do you exercise?

1 SNAPSHOT

Top six sports and fitness activities for teenagers in the United States	MALES	FEMALES
	1. Football	1. Swimming
	2. Basketball	2. Basketball
	3. Weight training	3. Bicycling
	4. Jogging	4. Aerobics
	5. Bicycling	5. Jogging
	6. Swimming	6. Regular fitness program

Source: *America's Youth in the 1990s;* George H. Gallup International Institute

Talk about these questions.

Do males and females in your country enjoy any of these sports or activities?
Do you enjoy any of these or other sports or activities? Which ones?

2 WORD POWER Sports and exercise

A *Pair work* Which of these activities are popular with the following age groups? Check (✓) the activities. Then compare with a partner.

	Children	Teens	Young adults	Middle-aged people	Older people
aerobics	☐	☐	☐	☐	☐
baseball	☐	☐	☐	☐	☐
bicycling	☐	☐	☐	☐	☐
Rollerblading	☐	☐	☐	☐	☐
soccer	☐	☐	☐	☐	☐
swimming	☐	☐	☐	☐	☐
tennis	☐	☐	☐	☐	☐
weight training	☐	☐	☐	☐	☐
yoga	☐	☐	☐	☐	☐

A: I think aerobics are popular with teens.
B: And with young adults.

B *Pair work* Which of the activities above are used with *do, go,* or *play?*

do aerobics ....   *go bicycling* ....   *play baseball* ....
....
....

3 CONVERSATION *Describing routines*

A Listen and practice.

Marie: You're really fit, Paul. Do you exercise very much?
 Paul: Well, I almost always get up very early, and I lift weights for an hour.
Marie: You're kidding!
 Paul: No. And then I often go Rollerblading.
Marie: Wow! How often do you exercise like that?
 Paul: About five times a week. What about you?
Marie: Oh, I hardly ever exercise. I usually just watch TV in my free time. I guess I'm a real couch potato!

B Listen to the rest of the conversation.

What else does Paul do in his free time?

4 GRAMMAR FOCUS

Adverbs of frequency

How often do you **usually** exercise?	Do you **ever** watch television in the evening?		
I lift weights **every day**.	Yes, I **almost always** watch TV after dinner.	**100%**	**always**
I go jogging about **once a week**.	I **sometimes** watch TV before bed.		**almost always**
I play basketball **twice a month**.	**Sometimes** I watch TV before bed.*		**usually**
I exercise about **three times a year**.	I **seldom** watch TV in the evening.		**often**
I don't exercise **very often/very much**.	No, I **never** watch TV.		**sometimes**
			seldom
			hardly ever
			almost never
	*Sometimes *can begin a sentence.*	**0%**	**never**

A Put the adverbs in the correct place. Then practice with a partner.

1. A: What do you do on Saturday mornings? (usually)
   B: Nothing much. I sleep until noon. (almost always)

2. A: Do you go bicycling? (ever)
   B: Yeah, I go bicycling on Saturdays. (often)

3. A: How often do you play sports? (usually)
   B: Well, I play tennis. (twice a week)

4. A: What do you do after class? (usually)
   B: I go out with my classmates. (about three times a week)

5. A: How often do you exercise? (usually)
   B: I exercise. (seldom)

B *Pair work* Take turns asking the questions in part A.
Give your own information when answering.

5 PRONUNCIATION *Sentence stress*

A 🔊 Listen to the syllables stressed in each sentence. Notice that the adverbs of frequency are stressed. Then practice the sentences.

I hardly **év**er do **yó**ga in the **mórn**ing.
I **óf**ten go **Ró**llerblading on **Sá**turdays.
I almost **ál**ways play **tén**nis on **wéek**ends.

B *Pair work* Write four sentences about yourself using adverbs of frequency. Then take turns saying the sentences using the correct stress.

6 FITNESS POLL

A *Group work* Take a poll in your group. One person takes notes. Take turns asking each person these questions.

1. Do you have a regular fitness program? How often do you exercise?

2. Do you ever go to a gym? How often do you go? What do you do there?

3. Do you play any sports? How often do you play?

4. How often do you take long walks? Where do you go?

5. What else do you do to keep fit?

B *Group work* Study the results of the poll. Who in your group has a good fitness program?

7 LISTENING

  🔊 Listen to what Ted, Wanda, and Kim like to do in the evening. Complete the chart.

	Favorite activity	How often?
Ted	....	....
Wanda	....	....
Kim	....	....

8 **WRITING** *Favorite activities*

A Write about your favorite activities.

I love to exercise. I usually work out every day. I get up early in the morning and go running for about an hour. Then I often go to the gym and do aerobics. Sometimes I go for a walk in the afternoon. About once a week, I play basketball.

B *Group work* Take turns reading your compositions. Then answer any questions from the group.

9 **CONVERSATION** *Describing exercise*

 Listen and practice.

Rod: You're in great shape, Keith. Do you work out at a gym?
Keith: Yeah, I do. I guess I'm a real fitness freak.
Rod: So, how often do you work out?
Keith: Well, I do aerobics every day after work. And then I play racquetball.
Rod: Say, I like racquetball, too.
Keith: Oh, do you want to play sometime?
Rod: Uh, . . . how well do you play?
Keith: Pretty well, I guess.
Rod: Well, all right. But I'm not very good.
Keith: No problem, Rod. I won't play too hard.

10 LISTENING

CLASS AUDIO ONLY ▶ Listen to John, Anne, and Phil discuss sports and exercise. Which one is a couch potato? a fitness freak? a sports fanatic?

a couch potato

a fitness freak

a sports fanatic

1. .... 2. .... 3. ....

11 GRAMMAR FOCUS

interchange 6

Fitness quiz
Find out how fit you are. Turn to page IC-8.

Questions with how; short answers

How often do you work out?	Twice a week. Not very often.
How much time do you spend at the gym? **How long** do you spend working out?	Around two hours a day. I don't work out.
How well do you play racquetball?	Pretty well. About average, I guess. Not very well.
How good are you at sports?	I'm pretty good at sports. I guess I'm OK. Not too good.

A Complete these questions. Practice with a partner. Then write four more questions.

1. A: .... at volleyball?
   B: I guess I'm pretty good.

2. A: .... swim?
   B: Not very well, but I'd like to learn to swim better.

3. A: .... watch sports?
   B: Pretty often. About three or four times a week.

4. A: .... spend exercising?
   B: I spend about an hour every day.

B *Group work* Take turns asking the questions in part A and your own questions. Give your own information when answering.

Who in your group is a couch potato? a fitness freak? a sports fanatic?

12 *READING*

Smart *Moves*

Look at the statements in part A below. Which do you think are true?

It won't surprise fitness freaks to learn that aerobic exercise does more than raise the heart rate: It lifts the spirit and builds confidence. But many brain researchers believe that something else happens, too. Just as exercise makes the bones, muscles, heart, and lungs stronger, researchers think that it also strengthens important parts of the brain.

Research suggests that aerobic exercise helps you learn new things and remember old information better. Aerobic exercise sends more blood to the brain and it also feeds the brain with substances that develop new nerve connections. If the exercise has complicated movements like dance steps or basketball moves, the brain produces even more nerve connections – the more connections, the better the brain can process all kinds of information.

Scientists still don't fully understand the relationship between exercise and brain power. For the moment, people just have to trust that exercise is helping them to learn or remember. Scientific research clearly shows, however, that three or more workouts a week are good for you. A study in the *Journal of the American Medical Association,* for example, shows that walking four to five miles (6.5 to 8 km) an hour for 45 minutes five times a week helps you live longer. So don't be a couch potato. Get out there and do something!

A *Pair work* According to the article, which of these statements are probably true? Check (✓) the statements. What information helped you determine this? Underline the information in the article.

Exercise . . .

1. makes you feel happier.   ☐
2. makes you feel more self-confident. ☐
3. strengthens the body.   ☐
4. can increase your height.   ☐

5. can help you learn things better. ☐
6. helps you remember things better. ☐
7. gives you better eyesight.   ☐
8. helps you live longer.   ☐

B *Pair work* Talk about these questions. Explain your answers.

1. Do you think that exercise helps people to learn and remember better?
2. Can you think of other benefits from exercise?
3. What benefits are most important to you?

7 We had a great time!

1 SNAPSHOT

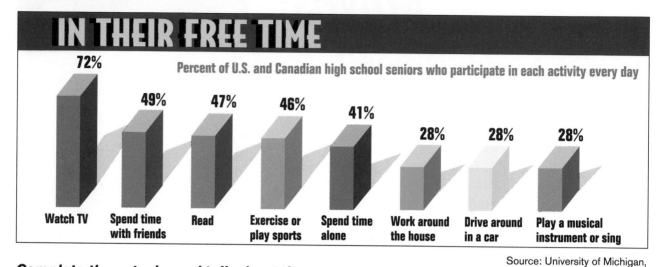

IN THEIR FREE TIME

Percent of U.S. and Canadian high school seniors who participate in each activity every day

72%	49%	47%	46%	41%	28%	28%	28%
Watch TV	Spend time with friends	Read	Exercise or play sports	Spend time alone	Work around the house	Drive around in a car	Play a musical instrument or sing

Source: University of Michigan, Institute for Social Research

Complete these tasks and talk about them.

Which of these activities do you do every day?
List three other activities you like to do almost every day.
Put the activities you do in order: from the most interesting to the least interesting.

2 CONVERSATION *The weekend*

A Listen and practice.

Chris: So, what did you do this weekend, Kate?
Kate: Oh, Diane and I went for a drive in the country on Saturday.
Chris: That sounds nice. Where did you go?
Kate: We drove to the lake and had a picnic. We had a great time! How about you? Did you do anything special?
Chris: Not really. I just worked on my car all day.
Kate: That old thing! Why don't you just buy a new one?
Chris: But then what would I do every weekend?

 B Listen to Kate talk about her activities on Sunday.

1. What did she do?
2. Where did she go?

40

3 GRAMMAR FOCUS

Past tense 💿

Did you **stay** home on Sunday?	Yes, I **did**. I **watched** a football game on TV. No, I **didn't**. I **invited** friends out to dinner.	**Regular verbs** invite → invit**ed** work → work**ed** stay → stay**ed** study → stud**ied**
What **did** you **do** on Saturday?	I **worked** on my car. I **stayed** home and **studied**.	
Did you **do** anything special?	Yes, I **did**. I **drove** to the lake. No, I **didn't**. I **had** to baby-sit.	**Irregular verbs** drive → **drove** go → **went** have → **had**
Where **did** you **go** on Sunday?	I **saw** a good movie. I **went** to a concert.	see → **saw** spend → **spent**

For a list of irregular past forms and pronunciation rules for
regular past forms, see the appendix at the back of the book.

A Complete these conversations. Then practice with a partner.

1. A: .... you .... (go) out on Friday night?
   B: No, I .... I .... (invite) friends over,
   and I .... (cook) dinner for them.

2. A: How .... you .... (spend) your last birthday?
   B: I .... (have) a party. Everyone .... (enjoy) it,
   but the neighbors .... (complain) about the noise.

3. A: What .... you .... (do) last night?
   B: I .... (go) to the new Tom Cruise film.
   I .... (love) it!

4. A: .... you .... (do) anything special over the weekend?
   B: Yes, I .... I .... (go) shopping. Unfortunately,
   I .... (spend) all my money. Now I'm broke!

B *Pair work* Take turns asking the questions in part A.
Give your own information when answering.

4 PRONUNCIATION *Reduced forms of* did you

A 💿 Listen and practice. Notice how **did you** is reduced in
the following questions.

[dɪdʒə]
Did you have a good time?

[wədɪdʒə]
What did you do last night?

B *Pair work* Practice the questions in the grammar box in Exercise 3.
Pay attention to the pronunciation of **did you**.

5 WORD POWER Collocation

A Find two other words or phrases from the list that are usually paired with each verb.

| an art exhibition | a vacation | a party | a trip | shopping |
| a lot of fun | the dishes | dancing | a play | the laundry |

did	*housework*	....	....
went	*swimming*	....	....
had	*a good time*	....	....
saw	*a movie*	....	....
took	*a day off*	....	....

B Write five sentences using words from the list.

I saw a movie last weekend.

6 ANY QUESTIONS?

Group work Take turns. One student makes a statement about the weekend. Other students ask questions. Each student answers at least four questions.

A: I went dancing on Saturday night.
B: **Where** did you go?
A: To the Rock-it Club.
C: **Who** did you go with?
A: I went with my brother.
D: **What time** did you go?
A: We went at around 10:00.
E: **How** did you like it?
A: . . .

7 LISTENING

  A Listen to John and Laura describe what they did last night. Check (✓) the correct information about each person.

  B Listen to the conversation again. What did each person do? Take notes. Then take turns telling their stories to a partner.

	John	Laura
had a boring time	☐	☐
had a good time	☐	☐
met someone interesting	☐	☐
got home late	☐	☐

8 *CONVERSATION* On vacation

🔊 Listen and practice.

Mike: Hi, Celia! How was your trip to the United States?
Celia: It was terrific. I really enjoyed it.
Mike: Great. How long were you away?
Celia: I was there for about three weeks.
Mike: That's a long time! Was the weather OK?
Celia: Yes, most of the time. But it snowed a lot in Chicago.
Mike: So, what was the best thing about your trip?
Celia: Oh, that's difficult to say. But I guess I liked Nashville the best.

Chicago

Nashville

9 *GRAMMAR FOCUS*

Past tense of be 🔊		
Were you away last week?	Yes, I **was**.	***Contractions***
Was your brother away . . . ?	No, he **wasn't**.	was not = **wasn't**
Were you and your sister away . . . ?	Yes, we **were**.	were not = **weren't**
Were your parents away . . . ?	No, they **weren't**.	
How long **were** you away?	I **was** away for three weeks.	
How **was** your vacation?	It **was** terrific!	

Complete these conversations. Then practice with a partner.

1. A: How long .... your parents in Europe?
   B: They .... there for a month.
   A: .... they in London the whole time?
   B: No, they .... They also went to Paris and Madrid.

2. A: .... you away last weekend?
   B: Yes, I .... I .... in San Francisco.
   A: How .... it?
   B: It .... great!
   A: How .... the weather?
   B: Oh, it .... foggy and cool as usual.

3. A: I .... in Istanbul last summer.
   B: Really? How long .... you there?
   A: For six weeks.
   B: .... you there on business or on vacation?
   A: I .... there on business.

Istanbul
London
San Francisco

10 VACATIONS

A *Group work* Take turns talking about vacations.
Ask these questions and others of your own.

Where did you spend your last vacation?
How long were you away?
Were you with your family?
What did you do there?

How was the weather? the food?
Did you buy anything?
Do you want to go there again?

B *Class activity* Who in your group had the most
interesting vacation? Tell the class who and why.

Vacation photos
Use the vacation photos
to tell a story. Student A
turns to page IC-9.
Student B turns
to page IC-10.

11 LISTENING

Listen to Jason and Barbara talk about their vacations.
Complete the chart.

	Vacation place	Enjoyed it?		Reason(s)
		Yes	**No**	
Jason	....	☐	☐	....
Barbara	....	☐	☐	....

12 WRITING

A Read this postcard.

Dear Richard,
Greetings from Acapulco! I'm having a
great time! Yesterday I went on a tour
of the city, and today I went shopping.
I bought some beautiful jewelry. Oh,
and last night, I heard some Mariachi
singers on the street. They were terrific.
That's all for now.

Love,
Kathy

B *Pair work* Write a postcard to a partner about your last vacation
or an interesting place you visited recently. Then exchange postcards.

13 *READING* Vacation postcards

Paula,

I can't believe my trip is over. I arrived in Egypt just two weeks ago! I was with a group from the university. We went to the desert to dig in some old ruins. I didn't find anything, but I learned a lot. I'm tired, but I loved every minute of my trip.

Take care, Margaret

Hi, Luis!

My Hawaiian vacation just ended, and I am very relaxed! I spent my whole vacation at a spa in Koloa, Kauai. Every day for a week I exercised, did yoga, meditated, and ate vegetarian food. I also went swimming and snorkeling. I feel fantastic!

Love, Sue

Dear Michael,

Alaska is terrific! I was just on a trip in the Arctic National Wildlife Refuge. There were six people on the trip. We hiked for ten days. Then we took rafts to the Arctic Ocean. I saw a lot of wildlife. Now I'm going to Anchorage. See you in 3 weeks!

Kevin

A Read the postcards. Then check (✓) the statements that are true.

☐ 1. Margaret had a very relaxing vacation.
☐ 2. Margaret enjoyed her vacation.
☐ 3. Sue was in Hawaii for two weeks.
☐ 4. Sue got a lot of exercise.
☐ 5. Kevin spent his vacation alone.
☐ 6. Kevin's vacation is over.

B *Group work* Talk about these questions. Explain your answers.

1. Which person learned a lot on vacation?
2. Who had a vacation that was full of adventure?
3. Who had a very relaxing vacation?
4. Which vacation sounds the most interesting to you?

8 How do you like the neighborhood?

1 WORD POWER   Places

A Match the words and the definitions. Then practice asking the questions with a partner.

What's a . . . ?

1. barber shop ....
2. laundromat ....
3. library ....
4. stationery store ....
5. travel agency ....
6. grocery store ....
7. theater ....

It's a place where you . . .

a. wash and dry clothes.
b. buy food.
c. buy cards and paper.
d. get a haircut.
e. see a movie or play.
f. make reservations for a trip.
g. borrow books.

B *Pair work* Write definitions for these places.

bank	coffee shop	drugstore	gym	post office
bookstore	dance club	gas station	hotel	restaurant

It's a place where you keep your money. (bank)

C *Group work* Read your definitions in groups.
Can others guess what each place is?

---

2 CONVERSATION   The neighborhood

Listen and practice.

Jack: Excuse me. I'm your new neighbor, Jack.
I just moved in.
Woman: Oh. Yes?
Jack: I'm looking for a grocery store.
Are there any around here?
Woman: Yes, there are some on Pine Street.
Jack: OK. And is there a laundromat near here?
Woman: Well, I think there's one across from the
shopping center.
Jack: Thank you.
Woman: By the way, there's a barber shop in the
shopping center, too.
Jack: A barber shop?

3 GRAMMAR FOCUS

There is, there are; one, any, some 🔊

Is there a laundromat near here?
   Yes, **there is.** There's **one** across from the shopping center.
   No, **there isn't**, but there's **one** next to the library.

Are there any grocery stores around here?
   Yes, **there are.** There are **some** on Pine Street.
   No, **there aren't**, but there are **some** on Third Avenue.

Prepositions
on
next to
across from/opposite
in front of
in back of/behind
near/close to
between
on the corner of

A Write questions about these places in the neighborhood map below.

a bank	a department store	a gym	a laundromat	a post office
gas stations	grocery stores	hotels	a pay phone	restaurants

> *Is there a pay phone around here?*
>
> *Are there any restaurants on Maple Avenue?*

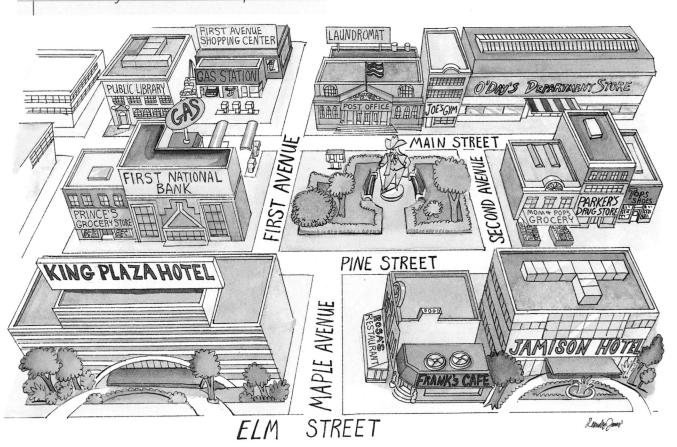

B *Pair work* Ask and answer the questions you wrote in part A.

A: Is there a pay phone around here?
B: Yes, there is. There's one across from the post office.

4 PRONUNCIATION *Reduced forms of* there is/there are

 Listen and practice. Notice how **there is** and **there are** are reduced in conversation.

There's a gym across from the shopping center.
There's a bookstore near the laundromat.

There are some restaurants on Elm Street.
There are some grocery stores across from the post office.

5 IN YOUR NEIGHBORHOOD

Group work Take turns asking and answering questions about places like these in your neighborhood.

a bookstore	dance clubs	a coffee shop	a music store	stationery stores
a gym	drugstores	movie theaters	a pay phone	a travel agency

A: Is there a good bookstore in your neighborhood?
B: . . .
A: And are there any drugstores?
B: . . .

useful expressions
Sorry, I don't know.
I'm not sure, but I think . . . .
Of course. There's one . . . .

6 LISTENING

CLASS
AUDIO
ONLY

 Some hotel guests are asking about places to visit in the neighborhood. Complete the chart.

Place	Location	Interesting?	
		Yes	No
Hard Rock Cafe	....	☐	☐
Science Museum	....	☐	☐
Aquarium	....	☐	☐

7 SNAPSHOT

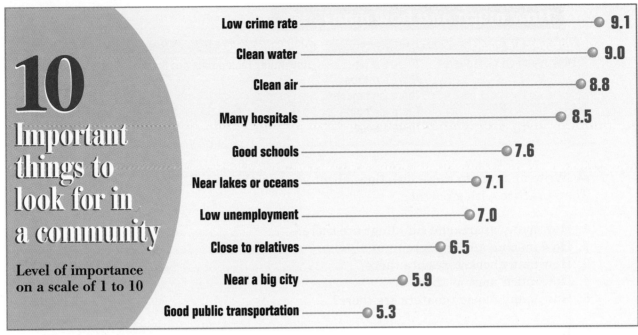

10
Important things to look for in a community

Level of importance on a scale of 1 to 10

Low crime rate —————————— 9.1
Clean water —————————— 9.0
Clean air —————————— 8.8
Many hospitals —————————— 8.5
Good schools —————————— 7.6
Near lakes or oceans —————————— 7.1
Low unemployment —————————— 7.0
Close to relatives —————————— 6.5
Near a big city —————————— 5.9
Good public transportation —————————— 5.3

Source: *Money* Magazine

Complete these tasks and talk about them.

What is important to you in a community? Rank the features above from the most important (1) to the least important (10).
List three other things you think are important in a community.

---

8 CONVERSATION *Describing neighborhoods*

A Listen and practice.

Dan: Where do you live, Kim?
Kim: I live in an apartment downtown.
Dan: Oh, that's convenient, but . . . how much crime is there?
Kim: Not much. But there is a *lot* of traffic. I can't stand the noise sometimes! Where do you live?
Dan: I have a house in the suburbs.
Kim: Oh, I bet it's really quiet. But is there much to do there?
Dan: No, not much. In fact, nothing ever really happens. That's the trouble.
Kim: Hey. Let's trade places one weekend!
Dan: OK. Great idea!

CLASS AUDIO ONLY ▶ **B** Listen to the rest of the conversation.

What do Dan and Kim say about restaurants in their neighborhoods?

49

9 *GRAMMAR FOCUS*

How much *and* how many

Uncountable nouns		Countable nouns	
How much crime is there?	There's **a lot**.	**How many** restaurants are there?	There are **a lot**.
	There's **a little**.		There are **a few**.
	There is**n't much**.		There are**n't many**.
	There is**n't any**.		There are**n't any**.
	There's **none**.		There are **none**.

A Write answers to these questions about your neighborhood. Then practice with a partner.

1. How many apartment buildings are there? ....
2. How much traffic is there? ....
3. How many bookstores are there? ....
4. How much noise is there? ....
5. How many movie theaters are there? ....

B *Pair work* Write questions like those in part A about these topics. Then ask and answer the questions.

crime   parks   pollution   restaurants   schools   stores

interchange 8

Neighborhood survey
Compare two neighborhoods in your city. Turn to page IC-11.

10 *WRITING*

A *Group work* Talk about where you live. Discuss these questions in groups.

Do you live in a house or an apartment?
Where is it?
How many rooms are there?
How much noise is there?
Are there any good restaurants nearby?
How many clubs/theaters/gyms are there in your neighborhood?
Is there any public transportation near your home?
How do you like it there?

B Write a paragraph about where you live. Use the information you discussed in part A.

> I live in a big apartment building in the city. There are two bedrooms,
> a living room, a dining room, and a kitchen. There's a lot of noise in
> my neighborhood because there's a dance club across from my building. . . .

11 *READING*

City Scenes

What are cities like in your country?

In many countries around the world, more and more people live in cities. Cities share many characteristics, but are also different from country to country.

Mexico Mexico's cities are modern but have traditional Indian and Spanish influences. The most important buildings are around a central square, which also serves as a place to meet with friends. There are outdoor marketplaces, where people can find almost anything they need. On Sundays, parks are a popular place for family outings. Many people move to Mexico City from rural areas. It has a lot of excitement, but also lots of traffic and air pollution.

Japan Japan's cities also have a mix of traditional and modern characteristics. There are tall office and apartment buildings as well as traditional wooden houses. Many people prefer to live near the center of cities, but because houses there are expensive, they often commute from suburbs. Traffic, pollution, and crowds are problems.

However, there is little crime, and even very crowded cities have many parks and gardens.

Australia Although 80% of Australians live near cities, the cities are not as large as those in some other countries. Most people live in houses in suburbs – not in apartments. The suburbs usually have their own churches, schools, and shopping centers. They also have recreational facilities. In large cities, like Sydney, the suburbs are often far from the center of town. Because many people commute to work, traffic is slow and there are many traffic jams.

A Read the article and complete the chart. Write one positive feature and one negative feature of cities in the countries described.

	Positive	Negative
1. Mexico	....	....
2. Japan	....	....
3. Australia	....	....

B *Pair work* Find five characteristics of the cities above that are also true of cities in your country.

Review of Units 5-8

1 DO YOU DANCE?

A *Class activity* Does anyone in your class do these things? How often and how well do they do them? Go around the class and find one person for each activity.

	Name	How often?	How well?
dance	....	....	....
play basketball	....	....	....
do karate	....	....	....
play computer games	....	....	....
swim	....	....	....
play the piano	....	....	....

A: Do you dance?
B: Yes, I do.
A: How often do you go dancing?
B: Every weekend.
A: And how well do you dance?
B: Actually, not very well. But I enjoy it!

B *Group work* Tell your group what you found out.

2 LISTENING

CLASS AUDIO ONLY

A A thief robbed a house on Saturday. Detective Dobbs is questioning Frankie. The pictures show what Frankie did on Saturday. Listen to their conversation. Are Frankie's answers true (**T**) or false (**F**)?

B *Pair work* Answer these questions.

1. What did Frankie do after he cleaned the house?
2. Where did he go? What did he do? When did he come home?

1:00 P.M. **T F**

3:00 P.M. **T F**

5:00 P.M. **T F**

6:00 P.M. **T F**

8:00 P.M. **T F**

10:30 P.M. **T F**

3 | *WHAT CAN YOU REMEMBER?*

A *Pair work* Talk about what you did yesterday. Take turns asking these questions. Give as much information as possible.

What time did you get up yesterday?
What did you wear?
Were you late for class?
Did you meet anyone interesting?
How many phone calls did you make?
Did you drive or take the bus anywhere?
Did you buy anything?
How much money did you spend yesterday?
Did you watch TV? What programs did you watch?
Did you do any exercise?
Were you in bed before midnight?
What time did you go to sleep?

B *Group work* Close your books. Take turns. How many questions can you ask?

4 | *ROLE PLAY* *What's it like?*

Student A: Imagine you are a visitor in your city.
You want to find out more about it.
Ask the questions in the box.

Student B: You are a resident of your city.
A visitor wants to find out more about it.
Answer the visitor's questions.

Change roles and try the role play again.

Questions to ask
What's it like to live here?
How much unemployment is there?
How much crime is there?
How many good schools are there?
Is traffic a problem?
What's public transportation like?
Are there many places to shop? Where?

5 | *WHAT'S GOING ON?*

CLASS
AUDIO
ONLY

A 🔊 Listen to the sounds of four people doing different things. What do you think each person is doing?

What's going on?	
1.	3. ....
2.	4. ....

B *Pair work* Compare your answers with a partner.

A: In number 1, someone is shaving.
B: I don't think so. I think someone is . . . .

Interchange Activities

GETTING TO KNOW YOU

A *Class activity* Go around the class and find this information.
Write a classmate's name only once.

Find someone who . . .	Name
1. . . . has the same first name as a famous person. **"What's your first name?"**	....
2. . . . has an unusual nickname. **"What do people call you?"**	....
3. . . . has an interesting middle name. **"What's your middle name?"**	....
4. . . . has the same last name as a famous person. **"What's your last name?"**	....
5. . . . is named after his or her father or mother. **"Are you named after your father or mother?"**	....
6. . . . always remembers people's names. **"Are you good with names?"**	....
7. . . . is from a beautiful city or town. **"Where are you from?"**	....
8. . . . speaks two foreign languages. **"What languages do you speak?"**	....

B *Pair work* Compare your information with a partner.

interchange 2 | *COMMON GROUND*

A Complete this chart with information about yourself.

	Time
I usually get up at	. . . .
I have breakfast at	. . . .
I leave for work or school at	. . . .
I have dinner at	. . . .
I go to bed during the week at	. . . .
I go to bed on weekends at	. . . .

B *Class activity* Take a survey. Ask five classmates for this information.

Names:	. . . .	. . . .	. . . .	. . . .	. . . .
What time do you . . . ?	**Times**				
get up	. . . .	. . . .	. . . .	. . . .	. . . .
have breakfast	. . . .	. . . .	. . . .	. . . .	. . . .
leave for work or school	. . . .	. . . .	. . . .	. . . .	. . . .
have dinner	. . . .	. . . .	. . . .	. . . .	. . . .
go to bed during the week	. . . .	. . . .	. . . .	. . . .	. . . .
go to bed on weekends	. . . .	. . . .	. . . .	. . . .	. . . .

C *Class activity* Compare the times you do things with the times your classmates do things. Whose schedule is the most like yours? Tell the class.

"Keiko and I have a similar schedule. We both get up at six and have breakfast at seven A.M. . . . ."

useful expressions

We both . . . at . . . .
We . . . at different times.
My schedule isn't like
anyone else's.

interchange 3 | *SWAP MEET*

Student A

A You want to sell these things. Write an appropriate price for each item.

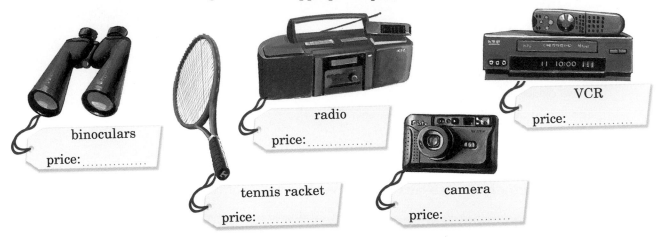

binoculars

price: ....

tennis racket

price: ....

radio

price: ....

camera

price: ....

VCR

price: ....

Student B

A You want to sell these things. Write an appropriate price for each item.

bicycle

price: ....

blender

price: ....

answering machine

price: ....

CD player

price: ....

TV

price: ....

Students A and B

B *Pair work* Discuss the price of each thing and choose at least three things that you want to buy. Get the best price you can. Be prepared to haggle.*

A: How much is the . . . ?
B: It's only $ . . . .
A: Wow! That's expensive!
B: Well, how about $ . . . ?
A: No. That's still too much. What about the . . . ?
B: You can have it for $ . . . .
A: OK. That's reasonable.
B: And how much is the . . . ?
A: . . .

* *haggle:* Buyers and sellers suggest other amounts until both agree on a lower price.

interchange 4 WHAT AN INVITATION! WHAT AN EXCUSE!

A Make up three invitations to interesting or unusual activities. Write them on cards.

Godzilla Meets Mightyman is at the Plaza Theater tonight at 8:00. Would you like to see it?	There's a dog and cat show at City Stadium on Saturday. It's at 3:00. Do you want to go?	I want to see the Turtle Races tomorrow. They're at 1:00 at the Civic Hall. Would you like to go?

B Write three response cards. One is an acceptance card.

> That sounds great! What time do you want to meet?

The other two cards are refusals. Think of silly or unusual excuses.

I'd like to, but I want to take my bird to a singing contest.	I'm sorry. I'd like to, but I have to wash my hair.

C **Class activity** Put all the invitation cards in one pile and all the response cards in another pile facedown. Shuffle each pile. Each student takes three invitation cards and three response cards.

Go around the class. Invite people to do the things on your invitation cards. Use the response cards to accept or decline any invitation.

interchange 5 | *FAMILY FACTS*

A *Class activity* Go around the class and find this information.
Write a classmate's name only once. Ask follow-up questions of your own.

Find someone . . .	Name
1. . . . who is an only child. **"Do you have any brothers or sisters?"**	xiao
2. . . . who has more than two brothers. **"How many brothers do you have?"**	l
3. . . . who has more than two sisters. **"How many sisters do you have?"**	
4. . . . whose brother or sister is studying abroad. **"Are any of your brothers or sisters studying abroad? Where?"**	
5. . . . who lives with his or her grandparents. **"Do you live with your grandparents?"**	
6. . . . who has a great-grandparent still living. **"Is your great-grandmother or great-grandfather still living?"**	
7. . . . who has a family member with an unusual job. **"Does anyone in your family have an unusual job?"**	
8. . . . whose mother or father is working abroad. **"Is either of your parents working abroad? Where?"**	

B *Group work* Compare your information in groups.

interchange 6 *FITNESS QUIZ*

A *Pair work* Interview a partner using this simple quiz. Then add up your partner's score, and find his or her rank below.

Fitness Quiz

Your Nutrition	Points
1. How many meals do you eat during a day?	
• Five or six small meals	6
• Three meals	3
• One or two meals	0
2. Do you eat at regular times during the day (not too early or too late)?	
• Almost always	6
• Usually	3
• Seldom	0
3. How many servings of fruits and vegetables do you usually have a day?	
• Five or more	6
• Two to four	4
• One or none	1
4. How much fatty food do you eat?	
• Very little	6
• About average	3
• A lot	0
5. Do you take vitamins every day?	
• Always	6
• Often	4
• Sometimes	2
6. Do you take more vitamins when you are sick?	
• Yes	4
• No	2

Your Fitness	Points
7. How often do you exercise?	
• Three or more days a week	6
• One or two days a week	3
• Never	0
8. Which best describes your fitness program?	
• Both weight training and aerobic exercise	6
• Weight training or aerobic exercise only	3
• None	0
9. How important is your fitness program to you?	
• Very important	6
• Somewhat important	3
• Not very important	0

Your Health	Points
10. Which best describes your weight?	
• Within 6 pounds (3 kg) of my ideal weight	6
• Within 10 pounds (4.5 kg) of my ideal weight	3
• More than 12 pounds (5.5 kg) over or under	0
11. How often do you have a complete physical?	
• Once a year	6
• Every two or three years	3
• Almost never go to the doctor	0
12. How often do you smoke?	
• Never	6
• Hardly ever	1
• Often	0

Total Points [ ]

Rank your partner.

55 to 70 points: Super job! Keep up the good work!

35 to 54 points: Good job! Your health and fitness are above average.

15 to 34 points: Your health and fitness are below average. Try to learn more about health and fitness.

14 points and below: You seem to be out of shape. Now is the time to start making changes. See your doctor or other professionals if you need help.

B *Group work* Compare your scores in groups. Who is the fittest? What can you do to improve your fitness?

"I need to . . . ."

interchange 7 *VACATION PHOTOS*

Student A

A *Pair work* You went on a vacation to Mexico and took these photos. First, think about these questions. Then use the photos to tell your partner about your vacation. Give as much information as you can, and answer your partner's questions.

"I had a really interesting vacation. I went to Mexico . . . ."

Where did you go?
How long were you there?
Who did you go with?
What did you do there?
Did you enjoy it?
Where did you take this picture?
Who is this/that?
Is this a . . . ?

B *Pair work* Listen to your partner talk about his or her vacation. Ask questions like the ones in part A about the vacation.

interchange 7   VACATION PHOTOS

Student B

A *Pair work*   Listen to your partner talk about a recent vacation.
Ask questions about the vacation and the photos.

Where did you go?
How long were you there?
Who did you go with?
What did you do there?
Did you enjoy it?
Where did you take this picture?
Who is this/that?
Is this a . . . ?

B *Pair work*   Look at these photos of your vacation in Thailand.
First, think about the questions in part A. Then use the photos to
tell your partner about your vacation. Give as much information
as you can, and answer your partner's questions.

"I had a really interesting vacation recently, too. I went to Thailand . . . ."

interchange 8 NEIGHBORHOOD SURVEY

A *Group work* Imagine you are looking for a new home. You need to decide where you want to live. Compare two different neighborhoods in your city or town. Talk with your group and complete the survey.

What kinds of people live in each neighborhood – families, young people, working people, retired people?
Compare the neighborhoods' recreation facilities, stores, schools, and public transportation.
How much noise is there? pollution?
What's one advantage of living in each neighborhood?
What's one disadvantage?

	Neighborhood 1:	Neighborhood 2:
people		
recreation facilities		
stores		
schools		
public transportation		
noise		
pollution		
an advantage of living in the neighborhood		
a disadvantage of living in the neighborhood		

A: What neighborhoods do you want to compare?
B: Let's look at Parkside and downtown.
C: OK. So what kinds of people live in Parkside?
D: There are lots of retired people. There aren't very many young people with families.
A: That's true. What about downtown?
C: . . .

B *Class activity* Study the results of the survey. Which neighborhood would you prefer to live in? Tell the class where and why.

Unit Summaries

Unit Summaries contain lists of key vocabulary and functional expressions, as well as grammar extensions for each unit. For Grammar Focus models, please refer to the appropriate unit page.

1 PLEASE CALL ME CHUCK.

KEY VOCABULARY

Nouns
back
bow
cheek
class
Dad
engineering
female
friend
greeting
handshake
hug
kiss
male
Mom
(first/last/full) name
nickname
parents
pat
student
(baseball/volleyball) team
women

Titles
Miss
Mr.
Mrs.
Ms.

Adjectives
married
same
single

Articles
a
the

Verbs
am
are
is

Adverbs
here
(over) there
too

Prepositions
from (Paris/France)
in (English 102/Canada)
on (the volleyball team/
    the back)

Conjunctions
and
but

Interjections
oh
well

EXPRESSIONS

Greeting someone
Hello.
Hi.

Exchanging personal information
What's your name?
    I'm .... /My name is ....
Where are you from?
    I'm from ....
How's everything?/
How are you?
    Not bad.
    Pretty good, thanks.

Introducing someone
This is .... /These are ....
    Nice to/Pleased to/
    Good to meet you.

Asking about someone
Who's that?
    That's ....
Who are they?
    Their names are ... and ....

Checking information
How do you pronounce ...?
    It's Mandel, with the accent
    on "del."
How do you spell ...?
What do people call you?
    Please call me ....
    You can call me ....
    Everyone calls me ....
Excuse me, what's ... again?
    It's ....
Are you studying ...?/
Are you on vacation?
    Yes, I am./No, I'm not.

Agreeing
That's right.
OK.

GRAMMAR EXTENSION Sentences with be

My name **is** Amy.
    be + noun

I **am** from Korea.
    be + prepositional phrase

I **am** Korean.
    be + adjective

2 HOW DO YOU SPEND YOUR DAY?

KEY VOCABULARY

Nouns
Jobs/Professions
announcer
architect
carpenter
chef
company director
disc jockey
doctor
engineer
flight attendant
(tour) guide
nurse
police officer
professor
receptionist
sales manager
salesman
salesperson
secretary
security guard
supervisor
teacher
travel agent
word processor

Workplaces
airline
(construction/
    electronics)
    company
department store
hospital
office
radio station
(fast-food)
    restaurant
school

Classes
business
computer science
mathematics

Time
day
holiday
hour
week
year

Other
clothes
country
(computer)
    equipment

food
high school
house
instruction
lunch
music
(news)paper
passenger
patient
people
phone
snack
tour
TV
weather report
work

Adjectives
average
full-time
great
interesting
little
long
part-time

Article
an

Verbs
answer
arrive (at)
build
care for
cook
do
get (home)
get up
go (to bed/to
    school/to work)
have (a job/lunch)
leave
like
love
play (music)
read
sell
serve
sleep
sound (interesting)
spend (your day)
start
stay up
study
take
teach
wake up
watch
work

Adverbs
a lot
early
exactly
home
late
only
pretty (late)
then

Prepositions
about/around
    (10:00/noon)
after (midnight)
at (night/7:00/
    noon/midnight)
before (noon)
for (an hour)
in (the morning/
    the afternoon/
    the evening)
like (Peru)
on (weekends/
    weekdays/
    weeknights/
    Sundays)
until (midnight)

Interjection
so

EXPRESSIONS

Describing work/school
What do you do?
  I'm a/an . . . .
Where do you work?
  I work at/in/for . . . .
Where do you go to school?
  I go to . . . .

Asking for more information
What about . . . ?
Which . . . ?

Asking for and giving opinions
How do you like . . . ?
  I like . . . a lot./I love . . . .
  It's a great . . . .

Expressing interest
Really?
Oh, really?
That sounds interesting.

Talking about daily schedules
How do you spend your day?
  Well, I . . . . Then I . . . .
What time do you go to work/school?
  I leave at . . . .
And when do you get home?
  I get home around . . . .

Apologizing
Gee, I'm sorry.

GRAMMAR EXTENSION

1. Prepositions in sentences about work/school

I work	**for** Toyota.	*for* + name of company
	for Ms. Jones.	*for* + name of person
	for a lawyer.	*for* + person's job

| I work | **in** a bank. | *in/at* + workplace |
| | **at** a restaurant. | |

| I work | **in** the sales department. | *in* + department/section |
| | **in** the front office. | |

| I go | **to** Columbia University. | *to* + name of school |

2. Articles
Indefinite articles
I'm **a** student.
He's **an** engineer.

a before consonants
an before vowel sounds

Definite article
I work for **the** *Daily News*.
    in **the** sales department.

the + specific place

KEY VOCABULARY

Nouns	*Materials**	*Other*	**Adjectives**	**Verbs**
Clothes and jewelry	cotton	adult	attractive	buy
backpack	gold	color	bad	get
bag	leather	compact disc	big	have on
boots	plastic	cost	cheap	let (me) + verb
bracelet	polyester	(room) decor	dark	look (= seem)
cap	rubber	design	different	look at
earrings	silk	dollar	each	pay (for)
gloves	silver	entertainment	expensive	prefer
jacket	wool	(for) example	good	spend (money)
(pair of) jeans		expenses	large	try on
necklace	**Names of*	(gallon of) gas	light	
pants	*materials can*	haircut	medium	**Adverbs**
ring	*be used as nouns*	health	nice	almost
Rollerblades	*or adjectives.*	money	OK	better
scarf		(birthday) present	perfect	more
shirt		price	pretty	right there
(athletic) shoes		salary	reasonable	
sunglasses		savings	small	**Preposition**
sweater		style	warm	for (you)
tie		(price) tag	yearly	
watch		taxes		**Conjunction**
		thing		or
		transportation		

EXPRESSIONS

Talking about prices
How much is this sweater ?
  It's . . . .
That isn't bad.
How much are those shoes?
  They're . . . .
That's expensive.

Comparing
The black boots are more
attractive/prettier than the
brown ones.

Identifying things
Which one?
  The wool one.
Which ones?
  The blue ones.

Talking about preferences
Which one do you like better/more?
  I like the . . . one better/more.
Which ones do you prefer?
  I prefer the . . . ones.

Getting someone's attention
Excuse me.
Hey.
Look!

Making and declining an offer
Would you like to . . . ?
  Oh, no. That's OK.

Thanking someone
Thank you (anyway).
  You're welcome.

Asking for more information
Why?
Do you mean . . . ?
Oh, these?

Expressing doubt
Hmm.
I'm not sure.

Expressing surprise
Are you kidding?

GRAMMAR EXTENSION *Comparative of adjectives*

Adjectives with -er
Add *-er:*   cheap → cheap**er**
Add *-r:*   nice → nic**er**
Drop *y* and add *-ier:*   pretty → prett**ier**
Double the final consonant and add *-er:*   big → big**ger**

Adjectives with more
more + adjective: **more** perfect
                      more expensive

For more information on comparatives, see the appendix at the back of the book.

4 DO YOU LIKE JAZZ?

KEY VOCABULARY

Nouns
Music*
classical
country
gospel
jazz
New Age
pop
rap/urban
rock
salsa

*Names of musical
  styles can be used as
  nouns or adjectives.

Movies
comedy
horror film
science fiction
thriller
western

TV programs
game show
news
soap opera
talk show

Entertainers
actor
actress
group
singer

Other
CD
date
dinner
fan
(baseball) game
gym
kind (of)
piano
play
theater
ticket
trumpet
video

Adjectives
best
favorite
new

Verbs
agree
ask
come over
go out
have to
know
listen to
meet
need
play (an instrument)
save
sing
think of
visit
want

Adverbs
just
really
tonight

Prepositions
for (dinner)
on (TV)
with (me)

EXPRESSIONS

**Talking about likes and
dislikes**
Do you like . . . ?
  Yes, I do. I like . . . a lot.
  No, I don't. I can't stand . . . .
  No, I don't like . . . very much.
What kind of . . . do you like?
What do you think of . . . ?
What's/Who's your favorite . . . ?

Giving opinions
I like . . . . Do you?
I can't stand . . . . How about you?
I think . . . .
We don't agree on . . . .

**Inviting and accepting/
refusing invitations**
Would you like to . . . ?
  Yes, I would./I'd love to.
Do you want to . . . ?
  That sounds great.
  I'd like to, but I have to . . . .

Making suggestions
Why don't you . . . ?
Let's . . . .
  That sounds fine.

Asking about events
When is it?
Where is it?
What time does it start?
Where should we . . . ?

Asking for more information
How about . . . ?

GRAMMAR EXTENSION

1. Plural nouns
Add -*s:*   singer → singer**s**
Add -*es:*   actress → actress**es**
Drop *y* and add -*ies:*   comedy → comed**ies**

2. Prepositions
Do you want to go out **on** Saturday?   *on* + day
Let's meet **at** the theater.   *at* + place
              at 7:30.   *at* + time

5 TELL ME ABOUT YOUR FAMILY.

KEY VOCABULARY

Nouns
Family/Relatives
aunt
brother
children
cousin
daughter
father
grandfather
grandmother
grandparents
husband
mother
nephew
niece
sister
sister-in-law
son
uncle
wife

Other
acting
age
college
exhibition
fact
family tree
headline
home
(foreign) language
lawyer
painter
percent
semester
theater company
winter

Pronoun
anyone

Adjectives
divorced
elderly
famous
together
young

Verbs
break up
end
get (married/divorced)
live
look for
move
remarry
return
say
stay
take (a class)
take care of
talk
tell
travel
visit

Adverbs
Time expressions
again
ever
most of the time
never
(right) now
often
still
these days
usually
this month/semester/
    winter/year

Other
abroad
alone

Prepositions
at (a university/home)
by (the age of . . .)

EXPRESSIONS

Asking about someone
Tell me about . . . .
What is . . . doing these days?

Exchanging information about the present
Are you still looking for a job?
    Yes, I am./No, I'm not.
What are you studying this year?
    I'm studying a foreign language.
Is anyone in your family . . . right now?
    Yes, my . . . is.

Expressing interest
Is that right?
What an interesting . . . !
Wow!

Disagreeing
Do you think so? I think . . . .
I don't agree.
I don't think so.
It's different in my country.
Not really.

GRAMMAR EXTENSION Present participles

Add *-ing:*
Drop *e* and add *-ing:*
Double the final consonant and add *-ing:*

go	→	go**ing**
work	→	work**ing**
live	→	liv**ing**
get	→	get**ting**
shop	→	shop**ping**

6 HOW OFTEN DO YOU EXERCISE?

KEY VOCABULARY

Nouns
Sports and fitness activities
aerobics
basketball
bicycling
football
jogging
racquetball
Rollerblading
soccer
swimming
tennis
weight training
yoga

Other
classmate
couch potato
fitness freak
free time
(fitness) program
sports fanatic
teen(ager)

Pronoun
nothing

Adjectives
good (at sports/for you)
fit
in (great) shape
middle-aged
old
popular
regular

Verbs
exercise
guess
keep
learn
lift (weights)
play (a sport)
stay
take (a walk)
work out

Adverb
hard
just (= only)
sometime
too

Prepositions
in (my free time)
for (a walk)
like (that)

Interjection
say

EXPRESSIONS

Talking about routines
How often do you . . . ?
  Three times a week/day/month.
  I don't . . . very often.
Do you ever . . . ?
How much time do you spend . . . ?
  Around two hours a day.

Talking about abilities
How well do you . . . ?
  Pretty well.
  Not very well.
How good are you at . . . ?
  I'm pretty good, I guess.
  Not too good.

Asking for more information
What else . . . ?

Expressing surprise
You're kidding!

Agreeing
All right.
No problem.

GRAMMAR EXTENSION Placement of adverbs of frequency

Questions
Is   he   usually   at the gym after work?
be + subject + adverb

Statements
He   is   usually   at the gym after work.
subject + *be* + adverb

He   isn't   usually   there on weekends.
subject + negative *be* + adverb

Questions
Does   he   usually   go to the gym after work?
does + subject + adverb + verb

Statements
He   usually   goes to the gym after work.
subject + adverb + verb

He   usually   doesn't   go on weekends.
subject + adverb + *doesn't* + verb

> *Always* usually goes between *don't / doesn't*
> and the main verb.

He   doesn't   always   go to the gym on weekends.
subject + *doesn't* + adverb + verb

WE HAD A GREAT TIME!

KEY VOCABULARY

Nouns
car
city
concert
(the) country
dancing
dishes
drive
housework
lake
neighbor
noise
party
picnic
trip
weather

Pronouns
anything
everyone
someone

Adjectives
all
boring
broke
cool
difficult
foggy
special
terrific

Verbs
baby-sit
complain
drive
enjoy
go shopping
have (someone) over
have (a[n] . . . time/
  [a lot of] fun)
invite (someone) out
see
snow
take (a day off)
work on

Adverbs
Time expressions
all day/month/year
all the time
as usual
last night/summer/weekend
the whole time
yesterday

Other
also
around
away
unfortunately

Prepositions
in (the country)
on (a trip/business/vacation)
over (the weekend)

EXPRESSIONS

Talking about past activities
Did you go out on Saturday?
What did you do . . . ?
How did you spend . . . ?
Where did you go . . . ?
What time did you go . . . ?
How long were you . . . ?

**Giving opinions about
past experiences**
How did you like . . . ?/
How was . . . ?
  It was . . . . /I really enjoyed it.
What was the best thing about . . . ?
  It's difficult to say.
Was the . . . OK?

**Making and responding
to suggestions**
Why don't you (just) . . . ?
  But then what would I do . . . ?

GRAMMAR EXTENSION *Sentences about the weather*

How was the weather?

it + be
It was cool/cold/freezing.
    warm/hot.
    sunny/clear.
    cloudy/rainy.
    windy/foggy.

it + verb
It rained/snowed.

KEY VOCABULARY

Nouns
Neighborhood/
Community places
apartment (building)
aquarium
bank
barber shop
bookstore
cafe
coffee shop
dance club
drugstore
gas station
grocery store
hotel
laundromat
library
(science) museum
park
pay phone
post office
shopping center

stationery store
street
travel agency

Other
air
bedroom
book
card
crime
dining room
idea
kitchen
living room
ocean
paper (= stationery)
pollution
public transportation
suburbs
traffic
unemployment
water

Adjectives
busy
clean
close
convenient
important
low
near
quiet
safe

Verbs
borrow
dry
happen
make (a reservation)
move in
trade (places)
wash

Adverbs
downtown
nearby

Prepositions
in (the shopping center/
    your neighborhood)
on (Pine Street/Third
    Avenue)

Interjections
by the way
in fact
of course

EXPRESSIONS

Asking for and giving locations
Is there a/an . . . around here?
  Yes, there is. There's one . . . .
  No, there isn't, but there's one . . . .
  Sorry, I don't know.
Are there any . . . near here?
  Yes, there are. There are some . . . .
  No, there aren't, but there are some . . . .
  I'm not sure, but I think . . . .

Complaining
That's the trouble.

Asking about quantities
How much . . . is there?
  There's a lot/a little/none.
  There isn't much/any.
How many . . . are there?
  There are a lot/a few/none.
  There aren't many/any.

Giving opinions
I bet . . . .

GRAMMAR EXTENSION

1. Countable and uncountable nouns
Countable

Singular	Plural
a bookstore	(**some**) bookstores
an apartment	(**some**) apartments

Uncountable

Singular	Plural
(**some**) traffic	–
(**some**) noise	–

2. *Some* and *any*
Questions
Is there **a** bookstore?
Are there **any** bookstores?

Statements
There are **some** bookstores.

Negatives
There aren't **any** bookstores.

Questions
Is there   traffic?
              any traffic?

Statements
There is **some** traffic.

Negatives
There isn't **any** traffic.

Appendix

COUNTRIES AND NATIONALITIES

This is a partial list of countries, many of which are presented in this book.

Argentina	Argentine	Germany	German	the Philippines	Filipino
Australia	Australian	Greece	Greek	Poland	Polish
Austria	Austrian	Hungary	Hungarian	Russia	Russian
Brazil	Brazilian	India	Indian	Singapore	Singaporean
Bolivia	Bolivian	Indonesia	Indonesian	Spain	Spanish
Canada	Canadian	Ireland	Irish	Switzerland	Swiss
Chile	Chilean	Italy	Italian	Thailand	Thai
China	Chinese	Japan	Japanese	Turkey	Turkish
Colombia	Colombian	Korea	Korean	Peru	Peruvian
Costa Rica	Costa Rican	Lebanon	Lebanese	the United Kingdom	British
Ecuador	Ecuadorian	Malaysia	Malaysian	the United States	American
Egypt	Egyptian	Mexico	Mexican	Uruguay	Uruguayan
England	English	Morocco	Moroccan		
France	French	New Zealand	New Zealander		

NUMBERS

0	1	2	3	4	5	6	7	8
zero	one	two	three	four	five	six	seven	eight

9	10	11	12	13	14	15	16	17
nine	ten	eleven	twelve	thirteen	fourteen	fifteen	sixteen	seventeen

18	19	20	21	22	30	40	50	60
eighteen	nineteen	twenty	twenty-one	twenty-two	thirty	forty	fifty	sixty

70	80	90	100	1,000
seventy	eighty	ninety	one hundred (a hundred)	one thousand (a thousand)

COMPARATIVE AND SUPERLATIVE ADJECTIVES

1. Adjective with *-er* and *-est*

big	dirty	high	old	tall
busy	dry	hot	pretty	ugly
cheap	easy	large	quiet	warm
clean	fast	light	safe	wet
close	friendly	long	scary	young
cold	funny	mild	short	
cool	great	new	slow	
deep	heavy	nice	small	

2. Adjectives with *more* and *most*

attractive	exciting	outgoing
beautiful	expensive	popular
boring	famous	relaxing
crowded	important	stressful
dangerous	interesting	difficult
delicious		

3. Irregular adjectives

good $\rightarrow$ better $\rightarrow$ best
bad $\rightarrow$ worse $\rightarrow$ the worst

PRONUNCIATION OF REGULAR PAST FORMS

with /d/	*with* /t/	with /ɪd/
studied	worked	invited
stayed	watched	visited

IRREGULAR VERBS

Present	*Past*	*Participle*	*Present*	*Past*	*Participle*
(be) am/is, are	was, were	been	make	made	made
bring	brought	brought	meet	met	met
buy	bought	bought	put	put	put
come	came	come	quit	quit	quit
cut	cut	cut	read	read	read
do	did	done	ride	rode	ridden
drink	drank	drunk	run	ran	run
drive	drove	driven	see	saw	seen
eat	ate	eaten	sell	sold	sold
fly	flew	flown	set	set	set
fall	fell	fallen	sit	sat	sat
feel	felt	felt	sleep	slept	slept
get	got	gotten	speak	spoke	spoken
give	gave	given	spend	spent	spent
go	went	gone	take	took	taken
grow	grew	grown	teach	taught	taught
have	had	had	tell	told	told
hear	heard	heard	think	thought	thought
keep	kept	kept	wear	wore	worn
lose	lost	lost	write	wrote	written

Acknowledgments

ILLUSTRATIONS

Barbara Griffel 15 *(top)*, 17 *(top)*, 18
Randy Jones 5 *(top)*, 9, 23, 29, 37
(top), 38, 46 *(top)*, 47, 52, 53, IC-4 and
IC-5 *(bottom)*
Mark Kaufman IC-4 *(top five items)*,
IC-5 *(top five items)*
Kevin Spaulding 3 *(bottom)*, 4, 5
(bottom), 14, 15 *(bottom)*, 28, 37
(bottom), 49
Sam Viviano 2, 3 *(top)*, 11, 17
(bottom), 26, 27, 31, 35, 40, 46
(bottom), IC-2, IC-3, IC-6

PHOTOGRAPHIC CREDITS

9 *(left to right)* © Jon Riley/Tony Stone
Images; © SuperStock; © Bruce Byers/
FPG International; © Dennis
Hallinan/FPG International;
© Michael Krasowitz/FPG
International; © Bruce Ayres/Tony
Stone Images
10 © Flip Chalfant/The Image Bank
11 © James Levin/FPG International
12 © Jon Riley/Tony Stone Images
13 *(left to right)* © Mary Kate Denny/
PhotoEdit; © Peter Correz/Tony Stone
Images; © Jeffrey Sylvester/FPG
International
16 *(top row, left to right)* Courtesy of
IBM Corporation; courtesy of Kmart
Corporation; courtesy of Kmart
Corporation; courtesy of SWATCH;
(bottom row, left to right) courtesy of
IBM Corporation; Jeans by GUESS,
photo © Richard Bachmann; courtesy
of Reebok; courtesy of Kmart
Corporation
19 *(left to right)* © Michael Keller/The
Stock Market; © Ed Bock/The Stock
Market; © Cybershop
21 *(top)* © Christian Ducasse/Gamma
Liaison; *(bottom)* © Alpha/Globe
Photos

22 *(clockwise from top)* © Fitzroy
Barrett/Globe Photos; © Alpha/Globe
Photos; © Paramount Pictures/Globe
Photos
23 A scene from *The Phantom of the
Opera,* photograph © Clive Barda
25 *(Bonnie Raitt)* © Alain Benainous/
Gamma Liaison; *(Cui Jian)* © Forrest
Anderson/Gamma Liaison; *(Caetano
Veloso, performing at SummerStage in
Central Park)* © Robert L. Smith
27 © Randy Masser/International Stock
29 *(left to right)* © Adam Scull/Globe
Photos; © Bob V. Noble/Globe Photos;
© Andrea Renault/Globe Photos;
© R. Henry McGee/Globe Photos;
© Imapress/Globe Photos; © Michael
Ferguson/Globe Photos
30 © Chuck Kuhn Photography/The
Image Bank
32 © Jim Cummins/FPG
International
33 © Rob Gage/FPG International
35 © Donna Day/Tony Stone Images
38 © Paul Loven/The Image Bank
39 © Kevin Horan/Tony Stone Images
41 © Michael Keller/The Stock
Market
42 © Peter Ginter/The Image Bank
43 *(ex.8, top)* © Gary Irving/Tony
Stone Images; *(ex. 8, bottom)*
© Hiroyuki Matsumoto/Tony Stone
Images; *(ex. 9, clockwise from top)*
© Zeynep Sumen/Tony Stone Images;
© Ed Pritchard/Tony Stone Images;
© Joe Cornish/Tony Stone Images
44 © Cliff Hollenbeck/Tony Stone
Images
45 *(top to bottom)* © Matthew
Weinreb/The Image Bank; © Wayne
H. Chasan/The Image Bank; © Joseph
Van Os/The Image Bank
48 © Schmid-Langsfeld/The Image
Bank

50 © Ron Chapple/FPG International
51 © Jose Fuste Raga/The Stock Market
IC-7 *(left to right)* © Chuck Mason/
International Stock; © Stephen
Simpson/FPG International;
© Michael Krasowitz/FPG
International
IC-9 *(top row, left to right)* © Cliff
Hollenbeck/International Stock;
© Bruce Byers/FPG International;
© Cliff Hollenbeck/
International Stock; *(bottom row, left)*
© Cliff Hollenbeck/International Stock;
(bottom row, right) © Cathlyn Melloan/
Tony Stone Images
IC-10 *(top row, left to right)*
© Telegraph Colour Library/FPG
International; © Darryl Torckler/Tony
Stone Images; *(bottom row, left to
right)* © Telegraph Colour
Library/FPG International; © Josef
Beck/FPG International; © Hugh
Sitton/Tony Stone Images

TEXT CREDITS

The authors and publishers are
grateful for permission to reprint
the following items.

41 Adapted from "Smart Moves," by
Susan Brink, *U.S. News and World
Report,* May 16, 1996, page 76.
49 *(Snapshot)* Reprinted from the
September 1994 issue of *MONEY* by
special permission; copyright 1994,
Time Inc.
IC-7 Adapted from "Lifystyle Quiz,"
by Linda Henry, *Muscle & Fitness,*
September 1994, pages 230–231.
Reprinted with permission.